How to be a
Virtual Assistant

Catherine Gladwyn

How to be a Virtual Assistant

Copyright © Catherine Gladwyn 2019

First Published in 2018 by Catherine Gladwyn

ISBN 978-1-5272-2224-3

First printed in the UK by Book Printing UK

Set and designed by The Book Refinery Ltd
www.thebookrefinery.com

A catalogue copy of this book is available from the British Library.

This book contains material designed to assist you in evaluating the merits of starting and running your own business for education purposes only. While the author has made every effort to verify that the information provided in this book is correct and up-to-date, the author assumes no responsibility for any error, inaccuracy or omission.

The advice, examples and strategies contained herein are not suitable for every situation. The materials contained herein are not intended to represent or guarantee you will achieve your desired results, and the author shall not be liable for damages arising there from. Success is determined by a number of factors beyond the control of the author including, but not limited to, market conditions, the capital on hand, effort levels and time. You understand every individual business carries an inherent risk of capital loss and failure.

This book is not intended as a source of legal or financial advice. You should always engage competent legal and financial professionals to provide guidance in evaluating and pursuing a specific business.

If you were to write your autobiography how cool would it look to add a chapter 'Successful Business Owner'?

How to be a Virtual Assistant

2019 Winner of VAVA Awards – 'Best Book for Virtual Assistants'
2019 Amazon Bestseller – Category: Small Business and Entrepreneurship
2018 and 2019 Amazon Bestseller – Category: Home-Based Business Book
2019 Mentioned in The Guardian – 'How I Spend It'
2018 The Independent Newspaper – Listed as One of Ten Best Business Books Written by Women

Contents

Introduction

Thank you for investing in me. It's not something I take for granted, so genuinely, thank you!

I really hope this book guides you to become a successful virtual assistant.

As businesses pull back on their expenditure and sometimes exploit their staff to do the job of not one, but many, employees may find themselves disheartened, unappreciated and underpaid at work.

I've looked high and low for the definition of work where it says 'unbearable, depressing, thankless, soul destroying', but it doesn't, because it's not supposed to be!

I've changed my working life to the point where I never actually feel like I'm working, and I want to show you how you can too.

You clearly want a better life, so I'm not going to waste your time or give you half answers. I'm sharing what is working for me, so you too can be a successful virtual assistant and lead a happier, healthier life.

I now often work less hours but earn double what I was when I was working full time and have the best work life balance I could dream of. Sure, I still get stressed, but never is it hard to get out of bed and never do I regret any of this journey. I am in my element.

And now, I want you to feel the same.

Ready? Exciting isn't it. *Let's do this…*

About You/Your Values

It's never too late to reflect and ask yourself, 'Is my life really how I want it to be?'

You may not have yet pinpointed the exact how or why you decided to embark on this exciting journey, but what I am going to assume is that you might:

> » Want a better work / life balance
>
> » Want less of a commute to work (bedroom to home office should do it)
>
> » Want to spend more time with loved ones
>
> » Want to earn more, but work less
>
> » Want to be your own boss
>
> » Want to get out of the rat race
>
> » Want to be away from air conditioned, noisy unhealthy work environments
>
> » Want to live your life by your rules
>
> » Want to take and pick the kids up from school every day
>
> » And most importantly, want more time for you

TASK

Whatever your motivation, write it down and stick it on your noticeboard on what will be your new office wall.

What is a Virtual Assistant?

When I first decided I was going to be a virtual assistant this is one question I found I couldn't answer out loud.

I had a business name, a website, business cards, a Facebook business page, a few networking events diarised, but I didn't have any spiel? What if the phone rang, what if someone emailed and asked how I could help them, what would I say at a networking event? I knew my role and what I was going to do, but how was I going to explain it to other people, especially face to face. It stems from my teaching days; I like to step back and make sure other people understand too. I needed to be able to grab and retain people's attention in a non-salesy, conversational way and you will too because people will ask *'what's a virtual assistant?'*

Out came the good old mind map.

I stuck a piece of paper on my noticeboard with 'Virtual Assistant' written in the middle and words to explain what I was and what I did coming out of it, similar to the image below. It was great to look at from time to time until I got used to explaining it to others without a blank look on my face. It gave me extra confidence. An older relative who isn't overly familiar with the online world might be a good one to practice on. If you're still struggling, how about asking a five-year-old for some tips, they seem to get this stuff.

Yes, you're effectively a PA/EA but virtual, people still often don't get it and that's good, it stops you assuming everyone knows what you do, because you're going to always want to be telling people, as we look at later in the book. It's like television dramas show a snippet of what happened in the last episode, to remind people and you'll want to be reminding people too. But more about that in the marketing chapter.

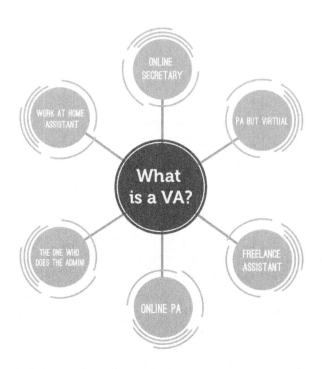

Personally, I try not to use the word 'virtual' too much, mainly because I get bored of fake laughing when someone says; *'but you're real'.*

Hilarious!

'You're a virtual assistant? But I can see you?'
(practice your fake laugh now)

A virtual assistant has become much more common place in the last few years, but you'll still meet people who don't know what one is, so it's good practice to learn how to explain what it means so people understand, are interested and see that you could be a huge benefit to their business when the time comes. Consider also being ready to adapt your response to whoever is listening, which is why you need to know exactly what a virtual assistant is and what you can do for people; e.g. a travelling business owner would benefit from knowing you can organise and manage travel and diary requirements with ease.

Finding Your 'Because'

Realising and identifying your 'because', the reason why you want to become a successful virtual assistant, helps you to stay focused, determined, motivated and resilient, among other things.

So, we are going to look at your *because*, your *why…*

My because was so I *no longer had to put my health and happiness secondary to work*.

I have Addison's Disease and take medication three times a day to keep me alive, it is also necessary for me to take an emergency cortisol injection kit with me everywhere I go in case I encounter stress (a fight, a car accident, a heated argument, for example – all things we can come across without warning), as stress can literally kill me within 20 minutes. Stress of any kind, happy or sad, makes me very tired and I have been known to sleep 15 hours a day if I haven't increased my medication sufficiently.

With that comes various hospital appointments throughout the year with specialists to help manage various symptoms and I found I was getting stressed just trying to manage those, let alone a home and family, and feeling guilty and stressed for attending appointments during working hours. My disease is just a thing, it's not my fault I have it. I've done nothing in life to contribute to it, so I shouldn't feel guilty. And neither should you feel guilty for anything.

Being my own boss helps me control my stress, thus improving my health and happiness and the happiness of those around me, and I can rest when I need to. The important thing here is health and happiness.

Based on my experience I view being an employee as being unhappy and unhealthy and that alone drives me every day to continue doing what I love and provide the best service to my clients.

So, what's your because? Maybe there's more than one?

Don't worry, this isn't a reality TV show, you don't need to have a life changing story, but you do need it to be primarily motivating for you.

Here are a few reasons some virtual assistant acquaintances of mine have given as their motivator:

- » *'To be able to take and pick the children up from school every day'*

- » *'So I don't have a two hour commute every day'*

- » *'To enable me to care for a relative at home'*

- » *'To secure my future' (employers can no longer be relied upon like they used to)*

- » *'To control my stress levels'*

And my favourite one so far:

- » *'Because I don't like people'*

If you're embarking on this journey because you see it as an easy way to make money, or because your mate is doing it, then it's not going to work.

Your heart, soul and every ounce of strength you can spare needs to be in it.

TASK

Pop your 'because' down and display it/them on that noticeboard.

Comfort Zone

Comfort Zone: 'A settled method of working that requires little effort and yields only barely acceptable results.'

Life can sometimes feel like you're spinning around in an empty room only stopping momentarily to catch a glimpse of your life then whoosh, you're back spinning again.

Sound familiar? Do you sometimes feel that days merge into one and before you know it weeks have passed and nothing exciting or significant has happened, or perhaps it has but you've been too damn tired and stressed to enjoy it?

That pretty much sums up how I felt working full time for someone else. Weekends were spent catching up on everything I couldn't do in the week, including cleaning the bathroom, washing, unwinding, smiling, laughing, seeing friends, then before I knew it, it was Monday morning again and I was back walking to work. And let's not forget Sunday evenings, you know the feeling, it starts getting dark and you start stressing or feeling sad about having to return to work the next day.

I guess I decided this was my lot, everyone feels the same, I can't complain I just have to get on with it. But that's not me. I'd had a bit of 'bad luck' if you want to call it that, so this wasn't my time to be hating every working week.

I wanted to make life better, but just like you, I had fears:

» Fear of failure

» Fear of going broke

» Fear of letting people down

» Fear of loneliness

» Fear of coping

Picture me in a cape, one arm aloft, full of spirit to change my life, but of course I'm scared. There are bills to pay, a child at college with dreams of going to university, I have an old house, the roof could collapse at any moment, I have a kitchen full of appliances that all seem to die simultaneously, like they've made a pact, we also love to treat ourselves to a cottage in Wales for our holidays once a year.

It's safer to stay where we are, isn't it? At my last job I'd been toying with the idea of leaving for quite some time when one day, after listening to a loud bullshitting colleague and the negativity of another PA, plus dealing with a boss who was drunk every day, I decided that I'd had enough.

To make a change we need to take some risks and step outside our comfort zone, that feeling of security. It'll either pay off and we'll achieve what we hoped for or it will form a basis for future decisions.

Pause for thought:

» Where's your comfort zone?

» What feels scary?

» Why not work part time alongside building your business for a while? I did.

Goals/Plan

What is a Goal?

A goal is the desired outcome from the effort put in.

As an example; the finish line in a race is the goal for those who are racing.

What is a Plan?

A plan is a detailed idea for doing or achieving something.

So, going back to that race, the plan is to start, maybe take in some water and keep going forward until you get to the finish line.

We set goals and plans in everyday life without even thinking about it, so don't stress about this stage of your business you're more capable of setting goals than you probably give yourself credit for. Just think of all the ones you set subconsciously.

- » 'When the kids are in bed I'll batch-cook dinner for the rest of the week'
- » 'When I've put the shopping away I'll reward myself with a nice glass of wine'
- » 'After the gym tonight, I'll pop on a face mask to totally relax'

Remember the last time you went out to complete two tasks... One to get the weekly shopping, the second to get some fuel. You subconsciously planned that journey, your time, where you had to be, you might have taken a list... You did it all without thinking, but it was still a goal and there was still a plan.

This journey must be about you from the start, as we agreed earlier in the book, so it has your full attention, your full motivation and doesn't become a chore. You've probably spent all your working life meeting other people's goals, this is now about you, it's time to enjoy your working days.

Why have goals?

Goals are used to help a business grow, develop and know it's direction. Setting goals is an important step in your overall business plan, so you know where you're heading and can focus, get excited and see what you achieve.

What are your goals?

To help think about and write down your goals you could use the following sentences as examples:

> By (date) _____ I will be fully operational with (number) _____ hours retained by clients every (month/week/day).

> Every (month/week) ____ I will publish (number) _____ of blog posts.

Whatever your goal/s, make them personal to you. If you have children you'll know that some new mums like to tell everyone their new-born has been sleeping right through the night from day one, that's not said to make other mums feel bad, it's to make the mums of these alien children feel better about themselves. So, avoid focusing on what other virtual assistants might be achieving, what their goals are, because you're unique and you've probably got a different end game.

You can have more than one goal, just make sure you're not reliant too much on outside influence to complete them.

And, it's perfectly okay if you need to move your dates forward, add to or change your goals, because, 'sometimes life gets in the way'. This is your journey, you're in total control.

TASK

Write down or type up what your goals are and pop them prominently on your noticeboard. And set yourself a date target, having a date to aim for not only motivates, but often helps prevent procrastination.

SMART Goals

Much like targets set by a manager for his employees, each goal needs to be SMART. I hated this business saying when it was first introduced into a place I was working, I thought it was just another acronym to remember and would bear no relevance to me getting the job done. I admit I was wrong, and I am glad I eventually came on board with them, as I too have used them in my business and use them subconsciously when helping my clients improve their procedures and processes.

SMART goals were first introduced in 1981 as far as I can see from some quick Google research, I can't personally recall as I was only four and thus too busy reading the exploits of Topsy and Tim. Now, if you've not worked with SMART goals before, it's great to familiarise yourself with them. They're also so important when receiving tasks from clients, it helps you differentiate between a clear task and a vague one that's going to be a pain in the backside.

So, you've guessed it, write SMART on your notice board.

S   Specific (What is your goal? Is it clear? Is it woolly, vague?)

M   Measurable (how will you know when it's achieved?)

A   Achievable (is it achievable, can you reach this goal? Or is it long winded and relies on other external factors beyond your control to be achieved, so you never really achieve or fail?)

R   Realistic (I want to be a millionaire by the end of the month. Hmm, it might be achievable if you are lucky enough to buy a winning lottery ticket, but realistically it isn't going to happen in your virtual assistant business. Make sure your goal/s are realistic, relevant and achievable with limited reliance on someone else.)

T   Timely (when do you plan to achieve the goal by? You may achieve it much earlier, or just after, but you need a date to work to otherwise it's open ended and you could still be shouting 'I'm going to be a virtual assistant' as they're wheeling you into your nursing home.)

By making sure your goals meet the SMART criteria it makes them so much easier to achieve. Goals are also more achievable when you're working towards a deadline and can be short or long term.

Initially your short-term goals might be:

- » **Week one:** Work out how much I need to earn as a virtual assistant.

- » **Week three:** Decide on what services I will offer as a virtual assistant.

- » **Week five:** Set up my business social media accounts by the end of the week.

Long term your goals will probably be centred more around:

- » Profitability

- » Client retention

- » Growth

These are all things I help established virtual assistants with, with my training and mentoring.

Business Plan

Before I go on, don't be disheartened by the term 'business plan.' You're not going to have to create a 50-page document, with graphs and projected figures for the next 5 years to enable you to open a business bank account. This is just for you. It can even be on the back of an old envelope if you want it to be.

Everything needs a plan. I liken it to being in a room full of escalators, all going to a different destination. You need to know where you're heading so you know which escalator to step on to, which way to go. If you didn't you could end up anywhere and it would be an anxiety filled journey.

Your initial plan, for example, may be one of the following:

- ☑ To be an employee part-time and your own boss the rest of the time for a six-month period.
- ☑ To earn enough to live on as your own boss within 12 months.
- ☑ To work a four-day week.

My plans initially were:

- ☑ To no longer be employed
- ☑ To work for myself earning a full-time wage
- ☑ To work from home as a virtual assistant
- ☑ To have a day off whenever I wanted without having to ask anyone

I know the last one might sound a bit daft, but to have a day off when I decide, not when it suits someone else's business does feel like I have control of my life.

Now I have achieved what I set out in my initial plan, my plans have evolved and are centred around:

- » Marketing
- » Learning (personal development)
- » Growing my reputation
- » Evolving my business as my client's needs change
- ☑ Writing this book! (check)

TASK

Whatever your plans, write them down because apparently, *'what gets written, gets done.'*

As a Successful Business Owner, You'll Need to be...

Grab yourself a highlighter!

You might be an exceptional virtual assistant, but you're also now going to be a business owner and with that comes a whole host of new, different responsibilities. Many, or perhaps all, you may slip into with ease. Others you may have to work on over time. You don't need to have nailed them all before you open for business but knowing what's going to be expected of you will help when things crop up.

I've listed some key traits along with a brief example of each, you'll think of others and you'll no doubt encounter more along the way, let me know when you do, I'd love to hear them.

- **Proactive** – to enable you to upsell yourself you'll need to be able to envisage what your existing and potential clients might need help with. This won't necessarily be instantaneous. As you get to know your clients you'll see what their day involves and what tasks they do, and you can offer to do them for them.

- **Resilient** – I promised to be honest, so I don't want you to think running a business is a doddle, I can't wake up in the morning and decide to take the day off, I still have bills to pay, but I can decide what time I start work, I can plan my workload so I can have a day off without having to ask anyone's 'permission'. I choose to have commitments to some of my clients, i.e. regular inbox checks, weekly tasks, etc., and that's something for you to bear in mind when you think about how you're going to work.

- **Confident** - never be afraid to ask a client to clarify a task. Ask questions, stick to your terms, your hourly rate and be confident in your abilities and business model.

- **Determined** – you'll find that when someone says 'I'm looking for a virtual assistant' that from under every rock comes everyone who considers themselves a virtual assistant or who is looking to be. You need to shine above the rest. Don't sit back, sell yourself... Stand out from the crowd, which we'll look at a bit more in the chapter titled, '*Finding clients*'.

- **Hard-skinned** – you'll get knocked back. People will not reply to your introductory emails, they'll be rude about your hourly rate or suggest you drop it, they'll choose someone else over you. Move on to the next potential client and just say to yourself 'that's business'. In fact, pop that phrase on your noticeboard.

- **Unapologetic** – this one's hard for me sometimes. I hate doing anything wrong and will often apologise when it's not even my fault. Avoid being apologetic for anything you do that's right, that was asked for, your clients need to be accountable for their shit too. As we'll discuss later, their lack of planning ain't your problem!

- **Genuine** – don't pretend to be something you're not, or something you think people want you to be, just be you! If you put on a persona people will probably see through it eventually and wonder what you're hiding, but more importantly you'll attract people you wouldn't normally attract and it's going to be hard doing business with people you don't gel with.

- **Honest** – this is so important in all aspects of your business. If you can't do a task, meet a deadline, be accountable when the client wants you to be, then say so. It's unlikely you're going to lose them, and if you do then that's better than stressing yourself out, agreeing to do something you can't and risking your reputation.

- **Accountable** – you will make mistakes, you will misunderstand instructions, you will get things wrong. We all do, for a multitude of reasons. Own them, admit when things go wrong, explain how you're going to ensure it doesn't happen again and move on.

- **Risk taker** – you're going to have to step outside your comfort zone from time to time to achieve results, to achieve your goals. It'll be daunting, but hell is it worth it. You'll have been a risk taker in many ways throughout your life, think of some now. Maybe it was buying your first car, your first home, deciding to care for another human being or animal. They're all risks, you didn't know how it would turn out, but it's something you wanted to do, so you did it.

- **Up-to-date** – sadly, being an efficient typist using only a typewriter isn't going to make you a successful virtual assistant. We all know how technology advances so rapidly. There's so much out there to learn and you're going to have to keep up-to-date with advances in admin and technology, among other things. I regularly create courses aimed at virtual assistants so you can up your skills and increase your list of services, check out my website for all the details – after you've read this book!

- **Relevant** – some virtual assistant trainers bang on about being able to minute take and earning a living from it. I'm yet to encounter anyone who's happy for you to take minutes regularly virtually, in fact it's damn near impossible because technology lets you down sometimes and it's hard to butt in to clarify any points. So, be careful what you excel at, consider whether it's relevant in today's ever-evolving world.

- **IT savvy** – there's no longer going to be an IT department to sort out your lost emails, your Outlook that will only open in safe mode or recover all your bookmarks when they mysteriously 'disappear'. You are now responsible for all those user errors and worse still, the non-user errors.

- **Passionate** – you need to be doing this for you primarily, there may be secondary reasons like spending time with the children, caring for a loved one, work life balance, health reasons, but this really needs to be about what it gives YOU because that passion will show through and your audience, your clients will love that.

- **Researcher** – you need to allocate time to read, learn and check facts. As I said, things evolve quickly and you need to be on top form at all times, so you can offer your clients the best, most efficient service.

- **Fact finder** – I see so many people turn to Facebook for the answer to a question. For example, how much tax do I need to pay? And they rely on whatever answer comes back that suits them. No! They should be visiting the Government HMRC website or asking an accountant, not someone on Facebook who is probably best-guessing.

- **Google proficient** – you're going to be all the things above, so Google will become your friend, along with books, experience and associates.

- **Manager** – you need to manage yourself, your time, your motivation, your diary, your workload. Can you?

- **Organised** – I almost forgot this, assuming you'd naturally be organised, but it's fundamental. Keep on top of everything! Even your own admin.

This list is by no means exhaustive, and I'd welcome your thoughts on additions.

TASK

If you're still an employee take your next working week to try not to ask a colleague or department for support or answers to any queries. Try and do everything yourself, because when you're in business it's all down to you.

TASK

Have another read through the above list and highlight all those things you can do with ease now and leave those you might need to work on blank. Are there any more you can add? Perhaps you could get some practice in now? Don't worry if it is all or most of them that need your attention, plenty of people have had to learn them all and you can too!

Building Your Reputation
(self-promotion)

You may find this part extremely hard, but if you look at it as another form of promotion then you'll realise it's not bragging, it's necessary.

Us Brits are taught to be humble and not show off, I think it's engrained at a young age where you avoid bragging to your peers at school for fear of a kick in the shins or being completely ostracised by your friends.

It's still not cool to start any conversation with, *'I'm better than everyone else, cus...'* but with a careful choice of different words you can show off and receive even more praise for it, which is something you'll have to learn to do if you think you might not be comfortable with it.

Firstly though, it might help to know why you need to do this and what the benefits are, before we go straight in.

There are going to be many products and services you've bought or invested in throughout your life because of other people's opinions and recommendations. Perhaps a family member has always used a certain brand, so you automatically did too? That's a recommendation in itself.

Brands brag about themselves all the time. M&S recently changed their logo to include their date of establishment, 1884. Why do you think they did that? The way I see it is this must be a brand I can trust, they have longevity, they must be trust-worthy to have been around that long. Can you think of any other brands that quietly but effectively brag?

To help promote you and the services you provide you'll benefit hugely from having other people wave your flags around and confirm you are as good as you say you are. Hunt down anyone you've ever worked with and ask them for a recommendation or testimonial.

Better still, have them write it on LinkedIn and then you can pop it onto your website and copy it into social media posts again and again and again. Contact ex and existing colleagues, bosses, voluntary associates and ask for a testimonial or connect with them on LinkedIn and ask for a recommendation.

Make sure the testimonials focus on your work, efficiency and are relatable to your new business and its services.

No good: *'Jane always dressed well and was often in the office later than everyone else'*. Who cares what you wore, you're virtual now, you can wear a tutu and tiara all day if you want to. Plus, as an ex-manager of a team of eleven administrators, I'd question why you were staying late? Incompetent or disorganised is sometimes the reason.

Good: *'Jane was really efficient at every task she undertook, especially producing PowerPoint presentations. Meeting deadlines and prioritising her own workload was something she did with ease'*. Better isn't it. It focuses on what you do well.

If you have people in your past who you know will take an age or never write a testimonial for you, because they're just not very organised, then write it for them, send it to them and ask for their permission to put their name against it. I know it might not feel natural, but you're just being proactive and efficient, everything a good virtual assistant is naturally. I've done this twice and I wouldn't hesitate to do it again. They'll soon come back if there are any changes they'd like to make or aren't happy. It's also a great way to let them know about your business.

TASK

Google how to ask for a LinkedIn recommendation, there's no point me telling you here as it might change, as technology often does, and ask for your first.

Ongoing Reviews and Testimonials

You'll possibly piss people off along the way, who doesn't, what matters is that you learn from it and then let it go. Or if you're not at fault, ignore it. Whatever the reason those people aren't going to be on your mind when you're no longer working, when you're retired and enjoying the fruits of your labour and that's what we're all aiming for right, so let it go and don't give them or the situation another minutes' thought. Focus on you, that's why you started this journey, for you!

Many of us visit TripAdvisor before we book a holiday, or Google before we make a purchase and some people check Facebook reviews before they do business. But, is one user's opinion really going to be the same as yours? If you see someone has bad reviews, you might look at those first and your clients might too. It'll harm your confidence, and you don't need that!

Facebook reviews. I hate them and turned mine off before I made my business page live. I've seen so many people leave bad reviews and the business owner hasn't ever done business with that person. Remember all manner of people use Facebook, and you're unable to control what they do. If a bad review comes in you're going to feel shit, it's going to knock your confidence and it'll no doubt be screen grabbed before you've even seen it. So, eliminate that nonsense now and turn them off.

I also check reviews and opinions before shopping or booking a holiday, but I appreciate they're subjective. One recent holiday cottage we stayed in, in Dorset, had one poor review because there wasn't a pub in the village? Why anyone thought that was the cottage owners fault is beyond me. Weighing that up against their otherwise perfect review history I decided I was going to 'risk' it, but it had clearly knocked the cottage owners for six and was completely unjustified given they'd never said there was a pub in the village anyway.

The cottage owners were determined our stay would be perfect, emailing in the run up to our holiday and even phoning us on the second day of our stay to make sure everything was as we wished. Lovely of them, but this isn't something they should be worrying about because of one person's irrelevant opinion, and you don't need the extra stress either.

FACEBOOK PAGE REVIEWS:
STAR RATINGS
Please read...

I recently tried to give a rating on a friends page, I hit all 5 stars (using ipad/mobile).

Unknowingly it gave her page a 4 star rating then a 1! (when she told me and I tried again).

What Facebook FAILS to tell you is you have to click on the 5th star first, but this is not made obvious. I clicked on all stars but started with the 1st star. If you do so it will only give a 1 star rating!

I am now very worried as have given many recent reviews, all I can say is if I have given you a poor rating please get in contact I didn't mean to do so!

25 February 2014

With all our Facebook Page postings today it made me give my Page a once-over. Has anyone ever looked at their 'star rating reviews'? We've had some fantastic comments with 5 stars, however my profile shows a lower rating.. Clicking 'see all' I notice several people (not customers!) awarding us 1 or 2 stars who have never used our services before. As we build our businesses on recommendation and reputation this is REALLY annoying! Has anyone else experienced this?

22 Comments

👍 Like   💬 Comment   ↗ Share

Blogging and Case Studies

Become the Expert

To be seen as the expert in the services you offer is a goal, it will enable people to trust you'll do a good job. Memes from Churchill and Einstein are all well and good, but you're not selling those, you're selling you and the services you can offer. You will need to show you know your stuff, that you can help, that you're confident and up-to-date.

You can do this in many ways, but two of the most effective right now are blogging and providing case studies.

Blogging

Blogging is, at the time of writing, a great way to share your knowledge, expertise and help others, whether you choose to do that through writing or video blogging – argh! The latter isn't necessary if you're not confident, but it's worth a try. You'll be able to judge what your audience will want to see.

Before you share anything always ask yourself who's going to want to read / hear this, who am I helping, what is this giving? Ideally, it'll always be the people you seek to engage with, your target audience, your future clients!

Your blogs will give people tips on how to make their lives easier, in a way that it shows your knowledge. Phew, that sounds confusing doesn't it.

Hang on, I'll break it down...

Before you start:

Think of the audience's pain point

(e.g. I can't manage the amount of emails in my inbox)

Write about:

Ways to help them manage their inbox, remembering that what comes naturally to you, doesn't come naturally to everyone.

(e.g. create folders, unsubscribe from newsletters you never read)

Prove you know that this works

(e.g. you have folders in your mailbox which help you to... You've put folders into other people's mailboxes, which helped them to... (Explain why it will help them)

What is the end result?

(e.g. they have a clearer inbox, clearer mind and a can identify the emails that really need their action quicker, so their competitors don't get there first)

Summarise:

(e.g. let me know how this works for you, or if you need some help with a mailbox spring clean, give me a shout, we can work together to make your life that little bit easier...)

See what I did there? I gave a little, offered some tips and then my call to action was for them to get in touch and not just in a 'spend money with me' way.

Call to action: *What is a call to action? It's a directive or instruction to your audience to perform your desired instruction, e.g. call me, visit my website, email me.*

TASK

It's a good time to think about your past jobs and consider what pain points your manager or the person you supported had, how you helped them and what you'd tell someone who also experienced that problem. You then have a few blog posts ready to write when time permits.

I tend to make my written blogs a minimum of 350/400 words and include bullets, headings and images where relevant, so that it breaks up the monotony of text. However, things change so rapidly, always keep an eye on what everyone else is doing so you're on top of your blogging at all times. I've not ventured into video blogs for my virtual assistant business, but you might want to. I'd love to see them if you do.

Remember: what's easy for you, isn't easy for everyone.

Don't worry about sharing tips on something that you offer as a service, e.g. how to create a spreadsheet for your mileage, you won't put yourself out of business, because there is ALWAYS someone who, no matter how easy you make it for them, hates doing it themselves, so they'll come to you to do it because you've shown you know your stuff.

I have a client who won't open his own post. That's fine by me, I love opening it, sorting through it, filing it and organising his office. He hates it, I love it – so it's a perfect match.

TASK

Write a blog on why you've chosen to be a VA – if it was so you can spend more time with the children, perhaps don't make that the focus as it gives the impression that your business comes second, and it may well do for you, but your clients won't want to know that.

Other blog title ideas:

- » How working with a virtual assistant can increase your productivity
- » What is a virtual assistant?
- » How do I work with a virtual assistant?
- » How to delegate to a virtual assistant

Case Studies

Case studies are a brilliant way to prove you can do something. I am sure you've been asked in an interview a question that started something like, *'think about a time when you did XYZ, how did you do that?'*.

I've got a couple of case studies in my blog section about how I saved clients' time by being more efficient in the way I work and only taking on tasks I know how to do. I saved one client £250 a month, so wrote about it. Take a look at it on my website, www.delegateva.co.uk

TASK

Think about a time when you've changed a process or adapted a task and made lives easier or increased productivity, no matter how small you think it might be, it's worth writing about to show off your areas of expertise, share your knowledge and show what you can do. Write it so future clients will want to work with you to do the same for them.

Maybe you made someone's life easier by adding lunch breaks or travel time to their diary?

Identifying Your Niche

This is something I found hard to understand and nail down to begin with; understanding why anyone needs a niche? Why I couldn't be all things to all people? The answer is, it helps to focus on the people you'd really like to work with, so you can target your content and services to them through your marketing. Ultimately this means you will enjoy what you do every day and be identified as someone who does XYZ and not just 'another virtual assistant'.

Your niche may be what you do, who you do it for, or a bit of both.

A bit of both

For example, if your background is as a legal secretary you're probably likely to look for legal professionals who need the support, because that's your area of expertise and hopefully what you enjoy.

So, your website content may read something like:

'After 15 years as a legal executive for a local firm of conveyancing solicitors, I now support legal professionals with all aspects of conveyancing admin. Including, deeds of assent, land registry searches, planning department communication, land charges, etc. ...'

And your social media content may be all about sharing latest changes in property law, conveyancing law, events aimed at lawyers, etc. Something that shows your interest, knowledge and that you understand your targeted audience's work.

What you do

Your niche might be what you do, for example, some virtual assistants concentrate solely on business admin and nothing else, which isn't industry sector specific. So, that's their niche. You may be offering social media management therefore your niche will be that and you'll promote that as a service, along with efficiency tips, testimonials around your niche services, to give further proof you're the virtual assistant people should be working with.

Who you work with

You may love to work with creative types, like artists and designers or you may enjoy working with people in the media profession, like journalists.

What departments have you worked in before? Maybe you worked in publishing departments and want to work with publishers and/or authors?

You'll have seen lots of business owners who have a niche, but may not have attributed it to that word, for example, people who choose to only work with women, that's a niche. I've even heard of a virtual assistant (in America) who chooses to only work with religious women. That's the beauty of being your own boss, you decide.

Think about your niche and think carefully about who you might be alienating by choosing to work with only certain people. Be mindful about who you're overlooking if your niche is quite defined, be careful not to overlook a minority, race, sex, etc. You are still accountable to the law.

The last thing you want to do it upset anyone, so be prepared to answer questions about why you've chosen your niche.

Is it an area of long-term interest or a trend i.e. only supporting women who offer video marketing? I'd be surprised if you'd be busy forever. Imagine if you ran a car wash, but only cleaned silver cars – daft idea isn't it? But it gives you an idea of things to consider when selecting your niche.

Whatever your niche, make sure it's something you enjoy and understand, so that you're a match for the client/s you seek. You may not want to be all things to all people further down the line, because you may attract people you're not enthralled about working with.

Some people mimic a trend or look at their competitors and go for the opposite, but you need to consider yourself when selecting your niche. Something you enjoy, something that'll make every day enjoyable.

Look only to your strengths – you might have always fancied working with medical professionals, but it isn't that simple! Medical admin is a whole different ball game, just like being a legal secretary. You need to know the jargon, decipher medical professionals handwriting and know where to draw the line. Lawyers and medical professionals rightly demand a high level of confidentiality from their staff, so they need to know you've been in that profession before and can handle the information you're going to be privy to. Registering with the ICO for GDPR isn't going to cut it.

There are a lot of people out there who aren't tech savvy, so need help with everything technical, like document formatting, etc. Great! Loads of potential clients, but the flip side of that is they are often confused or in denial about their skills and can be so bloody frustrating when they question why you've done something a certain way. I'm not saying avoid them, just think about every possible scenario before running with it and try it out quietly for a while before announcing it to the world, so you don't confuse your onlookers or look disorganised and uncommitted.

You may be drawn to a part of your current or last role that you particularly enjoyed being involved with. Perhaps you've read endless books on the subject, or even have a qualification in it. When you're comfortable with your choice then you can go forth and start marketing yourself to those who need what you have to offer - your target audience.

Niche for Life

You also don't have to make your niche all that you do forever. You're going to evolve, as are your business and other people's businesses, so you'll inevitably change and adapt.

You can always cleverly use words to promote yourself, something like this:

'I primarily work with marketers, but with a diverse background in... I can support any small business owner with...'

You don't have to tell people what your niche is, just target your audience or shout about your knowledge in your chosen services. Your advantage being, you know their mindset, their pain points, their needs and you've got experience in the things they're going to need help with.

TASK

Take a look at your work history on your CV and refresh your memory on who you worked with, what you did and make a list of everything you enjoyed, everything you were great at, qualified in. This may help you find your niche. However, don't spend too long on this, it's not a catalyst to putting the open sign on your business.

Networking

Face-to-face Networking

Understanding and being able to explain what a virtual assistant is and does is essential in a networking environment, as it's here you'll get asked the most.

One thing networking isn't, is a sales opportunity. It's about meeting fellow business owners, learning from each other and if business comes from it, then that's a bonus.

'I'm a virtual assistant'

'What's one of those?'

'Well, I support business owners with XYZ, but from my own home office not theirs.'

You can also promote yourself by adapting what you say you do so the listener can see how they might use a virtual assistant. If you know what the other persons business is, which you will if you ask, then you can adapt the response to the question to something like this:

'I'm a virtual assistant. Someone like me would help you with…., but I do it all from my own home office, instead of your office'.

The thought of networking can seem terribly daunting if you're not used to that kind of environment or you're not a conversation starter.

You're not alone, even the most outwardly confident people can be struggling inside.

At the beginning it's fine to step back on your first few visits. Don't worry about getting right in the middle of it all. Just put your phone away, smile and make polite conversation until you feel comfortable and want to engage and mingle. You're not going to lose any business or your reputation, nor will you self-combust if you take it steady. If you're confident and comfortable getting in the middle of conversations from the off, then do that too. You've probably paid to attend so you do whatever feels comfortable for you.

Many people recommend treating networking like dating and in some respects, I tend to agree. You shouldn't really go on a date with the hope you'll be married by the second one, and the same goes for networking, don't go there expecting to have a fully signed up retainer client after your first networking event, if you go there with that hope you'll likely feel disappointed and deflated.

I used to do online dating and I would always meet up with people with the mindset that I was going to meet a potential new friend, and if anything else came of it then that was a result. I was then 'rarely' disappointed, but that's a whole different book!

Many networking events allow you to attend for free a couple of times, or for a reduced rate before you're encouraged to sign up for a year. Some insist you go to every meeting and make a number of referrals throughout the year, or you're not allowed in again. Others let you pay as you go for as long as you like. I'd recommend attending lots of different meetings at various locations with different hosts, for as little cost as possible before you consider signing up long term to any, if at all. And get lots of feedback on them, if it seems too good to be true, i.e. we'll get you 50 new clients a year if you pay £500 (if such a group exists to exactly this spec, it's coincidence, I've made this up), then it probably is. Also, before you sign up to any long-term commitments consider that you will likely be seeing the same people week in week out, so if on your first visit you didn't feel great vibes look elsewhere.

Networking events are sometimes just coffee and biscuits with other business owners sat around chatting about stuff and not necessarily business. It's a great way to meet local business owners, have adult conversation and to get your face out there. You may go mad at times working on your own, personally I love it, but I did once comment on someone's lovely UPVC after a couple of days on my own while the boyfriend was away. I've walked past since, and their windows really aren't all that, so I must have been delirious.

Often at networking events people are invited to stand up and tell the group about themselves, others have speakers, some even have three course meals. If you stay local and live in a small town, you'll likely see the same people, as I did, so I ventured out to other local towns and cities, which certainly helped get my name out there, make some long-term connections and secure a few ad-hoc clients.

I decided after a while that I wasn't going to actively attend networking events as it's lost time and income and I had to weigh up the benefits. At the time I made my decision the benefit for me was staying in my office and building relationships online, which has proved to be the place I make my long-term client connections. I do not regret attending networking events in the past and will return when time permits, but I'll continue to venture out of town as well as in town. I may return to the scene, but at present spending 2 plus hours chatting isn't time well spent. In fact, it's £70 of my time, plus travel!

Dress code; dress in whatever you're comfortable in. Gone are the days when you need a black dress and heels and men need a shirt, tie and suit in my opinion. In fact, I wore this* to many networking events, it got me noticed and was a great conversation starter. (*See pic on page 54.)

*These t-shirts can be purchased from: www.virtualassistantshop.com

Online Networking

If you're not comfortable with social media it's best you get started because it's packed full of business people all day, every day! I know, it's not just employees who spend time aimlessly scrolling when they should be working. You'll not only find useful business contacts on social media, but you'll learn so much too.

Almost all my long-term clients have come from online networking. Facebook groups, my Facebook business page and LinkedIn.

While online networking seems to be free, i.e. you're not being invoiced by anyone, you must take in to account the time you spend online. Each hour is your hourly rate, it's an hour you're not earning, so you might want to ration yourself. It can be very distracting.

That aside, it's worth its weight in gold when you've become a familiar face. My clients will sometimes see a post for a virtual assistant in a group, recommend me and tag me in before I've even seen it.

Facebook groups (a modern way of networking)

Use Facebook groups to show your knowledge, share experiences, answer questions, congratulate people on their successes, mingle with people you'd like to work with and always be genuine. Many groups have 'rules' so make sure you read these through before you start posting as some things aren't allowed (i.e. self-promotion) and you don't want to draw attention to yourself for the wrong reasons.

Facebook and LinkedIn have business groups, which offer you the opportunity to identify clients, ask questions and learn. So, again rules permitting, share your own successes, blogs, dilemmas and tips, and ask questions that Google can't answer. Showcase you but give back too.

While these groups are an exceptional place to pick things up for free and learn about latest trends etc., remember anyone can hide behind a laptop, so always check what you've read / been told before sharing information someone in a group has given. Many people think because someone said it on Facebook it's fact, and that's not necessarily true. Much like celebrity 'quotes' in magazines, you have to take them with a pinch of salt unless you've actually seen the celeb say it or they've popped it on their own social media accounts.

Take some of what you read and learn with a pinch of salt too. There are people who are 'experts' in everything, but you need to follow up on their knowledge, their advice, question it until you see substantial proof. Seriously, it'll make you stand out and look less naive – a great plus for finding clients!

Likewise, don't ask questions that require an expert opinion unless you're sure of your source. As mentioned before, I see so many people ask questions about tax and accounting; imagine saying to the tax man, *'oh sorry I didn't think you were serious when you sent me that tax payment request 'cus this bloke on Facebook said I could pay it after my holiday'.*

So, to summarise, networking is vital, it's a form of self-marketing, but it doesn't all have to be done face to face if you're uncomfortable with that.

TASK

Search for some Facebook groups that cater for some of your personal interests, so if you're a parent look for a parenting group, if you like sewing, look for a sewing group. Join, see how it works for a few weeks and then you can start searching for business focused groups where you can meet like-minded business owners, potential clients and network from the comfort of your home office. I know, life as a virtual assistant just gets better doesn't it?

What Services Should you Offer?

This chapter is going to require stationery and we're going to do a little exercise. I am so excited. This is a huge step to starting (insert your business name here), but first I need you in the right mindset. No! That doesn't mean Prosecco and chocolate, I'm going to convince you that there are lots of services you can offer as a virtual assistant and none of them will ruin your reputation, leave you stressing or, most importantly, they won't cause the client wasted time and money.

Firstly, let's get that mindset and confidence in the right place. Have you heard of imposter syndrome? I admit I hadn't until fairly recently. The name gave me an understanding of what it was, and I dismissed it and thought, nah never had that. Until I read a little more about it.

Imposter syndrome is the act of holding back because we feel that luck, rather than an ability to do something is the backbone of success and that sooner or later that luck will run out and we'll be exposed as someone who can't do what we're so very clearly doing.

Even if you haven't heard of imposter syndrome before today, it's likely you've experienced it directly or indirectly at some point in your life. I've not yet suffered with this in work or business, but I've realised I did as a parent, so I do understand.

Imposter syndrome is not something to be ashamed of or embarrassed by, there's plenty of reasons why we experience it, many say evolution is partly to blame. As humans if we didn't carry an element of anxiety and self-doubt we'd enter every situation with a confidence that wouldn't allow us to see danger, so this imposter syndrome anxiety may well be a throwback from our early ancestors – we'll blame them anyway.

Secondly, as children we have an emotional need to fit in and belong in groups, which often leads us to play down our individuality or success to avoid being bullied or standing out in front of our peers to be mocked. It's different as an adult, we're actually more acceptable when we stand out and that's exactly what you need to do to be a successful, busy virtual assistant – stand out.

You too may have experienced it in some aspect of your life, you may have had an 'ah, yes I have!' moment when you read the above, followed by a 'that's how I feel when... I do an exercise class, I give friends advice, I teach my child something, when I go for an interview, reflect on my life so far...'

If you've not experienced it, you 'might' at some point, so it's worth us acknowledging it in case it rears its head.

Like I said, I had it as a parent for the first thirteen years of being one. I was convinced my daughter's academic and personal qualities were a fluke and that she'd turn in to a drug addict 'emo goth' at any moment because I believed I was a terrible parent. The worst part is she's a red head, so her pale skin would never suit the all black look!

Eight years on she's still not a heroin addict and has never dyed her hair, so maybe I did do okay? That's not to say I'm going to do it again, but I feel good knowing I wasn't a fraud. If you've been doing something well for a period of time, you're not winging it either.

So, we're going to shelve any thoughts of luck or fluke for this chapter at least. I know you can't just park it forever, but we've got to start somewhere... Ready? Shall we crack on?

Exciting! We need stationery for this one:

Please grab yourself a few sheets of A4 paper, your CV/ LinkedIn profile open, a biro and two highlighters, different colours.

With a sheet of A4 paper landscape pop three headings on the paper (Job, Task, Skill). You're going to reflect on every job you've had where you've done tasks that you quite fancy doing as a virtual assistant. Ready? Go...

Now, highlight all those you know like the back of your hand in one colour (just do it, because we've parked that imposter syndrome for now remember), any that are a bit iffy in another colour and everything in-between leave un-highlighted.

You may even ask a colleague or relative to check it over for you afterwards to confirm you've been honest and kind with yourself.

It's not just about your work experience, but your education too. If you've got a track record in success add it, and don't dismiss something because there was that time you made a mistake. You're human and if in doubt, blame your hormones!

If you're still employed, it might also be useful to keep a log of every task you do as you do it throughout a working week, because I bet there's quite a few things you just instinctively do without even thinking about it, that business owners would snap your hand off for you to do for them.

Your Services

So, we can definitely say you can add the ones you know like the back of your hand as a service.

The ones in-between too.

The third ones… Why do you think you can't add them as a service? Is it imposter syndrome kicking in again? I thought we agreed you'd park it!

In summary; the services you should be offering should come under at least one of these headings:

- ☑ What you love
- ☑ Where your natural talent lies
- ☑ Things you can do quickly (but others can't – time is money)
- ☑ Services in demand
- ☑ Your education and / or experience
- ☑ Services your ideal client needs

But remember, the services you decide upon now aren't the ones you have to stick with throughout the life of your business. You can add or remove them as you feel free, it's your business! Watch what others are successfully marketing and providing and get learning.

Also, the list of services on your website doesn't need to show everything, people will often ask for something unlisted and you can decide there and then.

What Services Shouldn't you Offer?

This section is actually quite exciting too, because here we're taking the first steps to you being in charge, taking charge and defining your services.

Let's take the summary from 'What services should I offer' and turn it around, so it helps identify what services you shouldn't offer as a virtual assistant.

- ☒ What you don't enjoy
- ☒ What doesn't come naturally
- ☒ Services that no one wants
- ☒ Things you're just not very good at
- ☒ Things you've never done before
- ☒ Services your ideal clients don't need.

What you don't enjoy

Remember those tasks you do / did as an employee? The ones that would sit in the in tray a little longer than others or those you'd telepathically hope your job sharer would pick up.

This journey to being your own boss means you don't have to do the crap jobs. Have a think about what they are so you're ready to say 'nope' when asked by a client.

For me, it's telephone calls. I don't enjoy them, so I don't offer it as a service.

What doesn't come naturally

Don't assume that just because you're a virtual assistant you have to offer everything a stereotypical PA does. If you struggle with logistics, then don't offer travel booking. I worked with a PA once who could not understand why she couldn't locate a tube station near Convent Garden, despite the email from the boss asking for train travel into Covent Garden.

We can't be good at everything, so identify those tasks from your list that you're really not confident with for whatever reason – imposter syndrome doesn't count at the moment remember – and scrub those off your list, for now. You may be asked at some point in the future to do something you aren't comfortable with, have little chance to say no and then realise you can do it confidently and can add it to your skillset. At the moment though we're not going to cause ourselves any stress.

Services that are dying off

There may be many tasks you love doing that not many people need help with or can't easily be adapted just yet to the virtual world, like minute taking. This is something that is really very hard to do virtually with a room full of people in another location and you on mute so unable to clarify things easily. Plus, many minutes (medical, children and adult social services, legal hearings, etc.,) need to be very confidential, so you being located elsewhere could have serious implications if your security isn't up to scratch.

Minute taking is an example, and I'm not dismissing it completely as a service to offer, but maybe add transcription services too, so people can send you their own recordings.

Things you're just not very good at

This feeds into the next heading slightly. If there's anything you're not very confident at, but really do enjoy, now's the time to refresh or build upon your knowledge. Watch some YouTube videos, do an online course, speak to people already offering that service, but whatever you do, don't blag your way through it. Please.

Just because you see other virtual assistants offering services doesn't mean you can too because you have the same job title. You don't know their background, what courses they've undertaken, or if they're blagging it.

Many virtual assistants like to offer social media management with no more than a little experience of sharing pictures of their children and dog on Instagram. You cannot transfer that 'skill' and become responsible for another business owners social media. It's not just your reputation at stake. There are lots of courses online, so learn and then offer the service. Invest in yourself and if you make the right investment you'll soon recoup the expense.

Many of the courses I write are designed so that you can learn new skills and turn them into additional services for your future clients, like my WordPress course, so the expense is recouped as soon as you start getting paying clients.

Things you've never done before

It's going to be so tempting to say yes to a new, or even an existing client, who approaches you wanting to buy more hours to do something you're not too sure about, but willing to have a go at, especially when you're just starting out and chasing the money.

Some people believe in faking it until they make it, even Sir Richard Branson is recorded saying in a YouTube interview on Oscar Guti's channel; *'I'm a great believer that if someone offers you an opportunity, whether you know anything about it or not say yes and then go and learn how to do it.'* Me, I'm against that completely. Learn how to do it yes, but I think Sir Branson would've had greater respect from me if he'd followed that line with; 'don't say yes to everything, don't lie about what you can do and never learn on the client's time'. I would never dream of giving myself unnecessary stress wasting a client's time or money by offering a service that I have no experience in. Remember, it's not just your reputation at stake but the whole industry and your clients too. I've taken over many clients from virtual assistants and social media managers who were pretending to be something they weren't.

Tell the client where your skill level is for a particular request and see if they're happy for you to learn as you go, or they may even train you themselves – you might be surprised at their answer given your honesty. Don't just wing it, please.

You could end up costing the client a lot of money if you get things wrong and that isn't good for your reputation or the reputation of our industry. I know I keep going on about this but being a virtual assistant is the best thing I have ever done in my working life, so I don't want anyone spoiling it.

I met someone who worked in social media, but they asked so many obvious questions. So, I did some digging, which wasn't hard these days and found they'd only ever worked as an accounts executive, dealing with invoicing for a large corporate company, but decided they 'quite fancied social media'. Turn that around, if I suddenly decided I fancied dealing with huge corporate budgets?

Services your ideal clients don't need

This is a difficult one to quantify, because there will always be someone who needs something you're able to do, but it's whether there's more than a few. For example, not many people need physical letters sent these days, instead people choose email or even phone calls – SHUDDER. Anyway, if your top service is 'letter posting' then you're probably going to be limited on clients and foreseeing the future, there will be little longevity in it.

Terms and Conditions

There are an enormous amount of freelancer / self-employed contracts available to download online, but if it's likely you're going to be working with just one client, then it might be worth consulting an expert to write a contract for you, to ensure it's as legally binding as possible and try and get a cancellation clause in there, to give you time to find more clients.

The following is what I do, not what I advise as I have no legal training.

Personally, I'm not overly hung up on getting clients to 'sign' a contract per se, but I do ask for an email from the decision maker to acknowledge they've read my terms and conditions and are happy (tell me if I am wrong, I'd welcome knowing). My reasoning behind this is that the e-sign process works by identifying people through their email address, so I see an email back saying 'all okay' as sufficient and as I run my business to alleviate workload for my clients, I can't be bothered with giving them extra work to do, and some aren't terribly computer literate.

Whether you choose email, e-sign or a written letter (remember those), here are a few things that would be worth including:

» Get confirmation from the decision maker that they agree to the terms of your contract

» Keep all written and electronic communication safe and secure (you never know when you might need to refer to this if there are any problems)

»   Stick to your own terms; if you don't why should your client?

»   Get everything established in writing, from the task specifics, your understanding of outcomes and the deadline.

You may well adapt your terms regularly, as different situations arise. I know I have. If you update your terms and conditions, be sure to send it to all current clients so they have the latest copy.

I have my terms and conditions available for clients and potential clients to view on my website, which you're welcome to view too – but not copy, that's plagiarism and illegal. I didn't write it completely myself but have written permission to use the original version of it. It's never been checked by anyone with a law degree, so you will need to take it as it is.

Consider this, if a client no longer has the need for you or the money to pay you, then they can end your relationship very easily, just like an employer can who's gone into administration, *regardless of any contract - be ready for any situation to arise at any point in your journey.*

Here's an example of how quickly a company can no longer be in a position to pay you and there's very little you can do about it:

I provided social media support to a company who had been in business for ten years, their product came with 'free forever' online storage, but there came a point when they were no longer making any profit from their sales by providing that, so they revoked it with 14 days-notice. Long story short, social media kicked off, online reviews turned very bad and they have been swimming upstream ever since to rescue what they have left of a business. By the time this book goes to print, I very much doubt they'll have a business at all.

Finding Clients

If you've identified your niche already this bit is going to be a doddle, but don't worry if you haven't, we can still crack on successfully.

Making Yourself Known

First thing we're going to do is announce you have arrived! You're a business owner, a virtual assistant and people need to know.

Invite all your friends and family to like your businesses social media accounts telling them that their support in your venture would be invaluable and if they ever have a spare moment to share your business posts with their friends, then you'd be unbelievably grateful.

This is also where you 'might' find some people are not very supportive and quite negative about your business venture, or you might not have that at all. I didn't, but I know people who have, and I want you to be ready for as many eventualities as possible. Now is a good time to surround yourself with people who want to understand what you do, believe in you and support your dream. Anyone who doesn't might need a little less of your attention while you focus your energy on being a successful business owner.

Pop a post on your personal Facebook page letting friends and family know you've started your own business and would love them to follow you on your social media platforms and tell all their contacts about you and include a call to action (i.e. add a link to your website, Facebook business page or LinkedIn, whichever is most relevant – more about that in the marketing chapter!)

Email relatives and let them know what you're doing and who you're aiming at and again include a call to action, remember not to overlook anyone. Also remember to personalise the email, ask how they are – and not the generic 'how are you' because even though you might not care deep down, you're going to want to engage them from the off and what better way than to get them thinking and talking about themselves, refer to something you both know about or have done together, ask how their family are by name and don't be afraid to let them know you're a new business and would really appreciate any free marketing they could provide, you can bet most, if not all, will be only too happy to be part of your journey, people like having a purpose and being part of something new.

» Reply appropriately to any replies you receive, thank them if they wish you luck or say they'll recommend you.

» Email friends and partners of friends and tell them too and again include a call to action.

» Avoid offering incentives for people to recommend you. Be recommended for what you do, who you are, not for what the referrer is getting out of it.

» Say hello to the world with your first post on the social media channels you've chosen and include a...*you've got it*...call to action. And as with contacting friends, don't be afraid to let the world know you're a new business, but with a host of skills and experience behind you. People love to support new businesses and enjoy watching you grow.

» Contact ex-employers and colleagues and let them know what you are doing, even if you don't think they'll need you, you don't know who their contacts are.

» Tell colleagues, if it doesn't breach any terms of contract. It won't hurt speaking to HR first and whatever they say, follow up with an email to confirm and cover yourself.

Want to know how I told my colleagues? I was very naughty but I've never seen an IT department move so fast. On my last day I sent an all users email to let everyone know what I was off to do, along with a link to my website. I'd had the email in drafts for weeks ready to send, checking it constantly for errors. People were so supportive and followed my social media platforms, contacted me via LinkedIn. It helped get my name out to people who may never have known. And, best of all, they couldn't sack me because I'd resigned! Hahahaha. Like I said, I'd never seen the IT department work so fast, they revoked my access in 10 minutes! I knew they could work faster if they really tried.

Anyway, I digress...

My first client, who I have worked with every month since, was the wife of a long-term friend. I knew she was self-employed but didn't know to what extent. I sent her an email letting her know what I was now doing, the services I offered and (I believe) gave her a link to my Facebook business page. I didn't expect anything from it, but thought it was worth telling her in case she knew anyone or had anything she'd like help with in the future.

I've learnt so much from working with her, her business model and ethos is amazing. She's a true delight and sending her that email was the best thing I ever did.

My second client was a lady I'd come across at my previous employer. I used to deal with the department's budget and she was a marketing consultant – her invoices were a right old pickle, so I made a point of getting in touch with her and offered to help her with any admin, sneakily mentioning that I have experience with invoicing and budgeting. She bit my hand off and we worked together for about six months sorting out her finances.

My third client was right place, right time. I had sent a load of local business owners emails outlining what I could help them with. One replied saying he'd been thinking about getting some help, so my email had arrived at just the right time.

You will find a lot of potential clients via Facebook groups. You'll see in many groups, for example, people put a post out asking if anyone can recommend a virtual assistant, what comes next is a barrage of virtual assistants all shouting 'pick me' or 'PM me'. If that was you looking for a virtual assistant, chances are your time is limited so what would you do with all those responses?

You'd either:

   a.   Respond to the first couple

   b.   Respond to the ones that stand out

   c.   Not respond to any because there's too much noise

   d.   Turn off notifications for the post and never go back to it

So, you need to stand out, you need to get at the front of that queue! Remember the traits of a business owner.

My niche is a sector - for example, the medical sector.
Start by searching for local businesses within your sector.

My niche are my skills and services – for example transcription.
Start by identifying which local businesses and organisations your services would really benefit. Search for the top bod on LinkedIn, connect and then stalk and pounce at the right time. Think about how you'd like to be contacted with a service that might help you?

I've not got my niche nailed yet
Start with friends and family.

Legal stalking

If you're on social media I know you've done it! That school bully, the ex, the criminal in the local paper. Well now all that practice can be used to stalk your potential clients – disclaimer: sitting outside their homes is not legal, apparently! One example where I pounced online and caught a client was when I saw a post from a lady in a bookkeeping group who was holding regular webinars. She posted that the next webinar would have double the usual participants so apologised in advance if she messed up the admin side of things, like sending people links to register, login, etc. Great of her to forewarn attendees things might go wrong, but it wouldn't look good for her if it did, would it? In fact, it'd look even better for her if it went smoothly.

I reckoned I could help with that, being Mrs Organised, so I hunted her down on LinkedIn, researched her website, so I knew more about her and her business, found her email address and sent her an email offering my help with her forthcoming webinar. I then followed up with a personalised connection request on LinkedIn, saying, *'further to my email, I'd like to connect on here too.'*

See what I did there?

- ☑   I highlighted my email so she wouldn't miss it
- ☑   I'd offered her help to solve her problem
- ☑   Been proactive

Imagine if you tell a friend you're really not finding your weekly shopping any fun at all and wish someone else could do it.

Boom, you get an email from someone offering to do just that, in fact they'll even check your cupboards to make sure there's nothing you've left off the list.

I was her saving grace, the webinar went smoothly, everyone got a link before and after the event and I have worked with her on an ad-hoc basis ever since.

Summary:

> » Put yourself in the client's mind? They're probably really busy.

> » Think about what would make someone stand out for you?

> » How would you decide on who to select?

> » How are you going to 'prove' you have the skills to be their virtual assistant?

> » Who do you enjoy working with?

> » Who would you not want to work with?

Identify, Agitate, Solve

This is how you're going to target potential clients and it's also something else for your noticeboard. Pop **Identify, agitate, solve** on there now.

Identify a potential client's problem or pain point:
The client: *'I can't cope with all my emails'*

Agitate the potential client's problem (kick them while they're in that mindset)
Your social media post / blog could read: *'There's another email! Do you read it now, later, tomorrow or in a few days when you've finished what you're working on? But what if it's urgent? Have they contacted your competitors?'*

Solve the client's problem with a solution
Your solution: *'Allocate regular times in your day to check your emails and*

pop these details on your email signature so regular clients know when to expect a reply. Or for those urgent emails outsource your mailbox management so you know you're never missing anything important'.

---

*Include a **call to action**, even if it's just a link to your website.*

Follow this up over proceeding days with blog posts, other mailbox tips, testimonials to show your expertise and efficiency in this area.

Following up

By all means follow up on prospects or let them know when you add further services, but don't bombard people. As long as your marketing is consistent and relevant they'll know you're there and when you see that they may need some extra help, that's when you can direct pounce again. Remember you're there to give them time back, not take it away, so always consider that before you contact anyone.

Sometimes it's a waiting game, but there's always something you could be doing to build and develop your business, like learning new skills (check out my courses over at howtobeava.co.uk), marketing yourself, etc. Think of those things now, write them down and you can refer to them during those quiet periods.

More than one Client

Always try and make sure that you have more than one client, this won't be possible immediately unless you bag two at once or in quick succession, which isn't unachievable – I had three almost immediately - but this would require an element of good fortune.

If you only have one client, what happens if they suddenly don't need you anymore because their own business has folded, or they've got a health problem, run out of money? How long can you survive with no income? How long will it take you to find a new client? How long's a piece of string?

Don't panic! Employees are in a very similar situation, if not worse! They rely on one person for their income too. On more than one occasion I've seen a LinkedIn post that reads: *'I've been made redundant today, available immediately'*. Once you have a plethora of regular clients on your books you'll be in a strong position compared to anyone who's employed.

I used to have a client who turned in to the devil client, and I was forced at one point to stop working with that particular lady. She had rapidly commandeered a large proportion of my weekly hours and remembering what I'd read before I started my business, *"no one client should take up more than 20% of your time"*, I had to call it quits. Before parting ways with her I made sure I wasn't going to be left in financial dire straits, by marketing hard for more clients, so it was an easy transition for me and stress free when I finally said 'C'ya!'.

However, if I hadn't been so prepared I'd have been in a panic situation and possibly contemplating becoming an employee again. Eww, that makes me itch.

TASK

What's your 20% in hours or money? You may be able to answer this one a little more easily after the chapter, what should you charge? When you know it, it's another one for the noticeboard.

Getting rid of a Client

There's also going to be occasions where you just don't work well with a client and you may decide you need to get rid. That's fine too, just remind yourself why you started your business… for freedom, happiness, less stress and more time. If anyone is stepping on those dreams then you need to put a stop to it. Don't apologise for wanting to be happy.

You can address the issues, suggest ways you'd prefer to work, or receive tasks or be spoken to and see if there's any change. If things continue in a way that's not comfortable for you, then it's time to be the boss of your business and end that relationship.

If you need to have a difficult conversation with a client, try not to procrastinate as your work may well suffer and they'll pick up on that. Have the conversation sooner rather than later.

I'd use something along the lines of:

» Following our chat on dd/mm/yyyy I'm still not completely clear on your direction or requirements or how best to proceed (delete as appropriate).

» Having considered this carefully, I believe that perhaps I am not the best fit for your business at this current time.

» I am happy to complete the *** task, but following sign off I will remove all documents, passwords and usernames from my systems for security and data protection purposes.

» I really do value the time we've spent working together.

There will be times when a client has completely peed you off and it'll be so tempting to tell them so, but I promise you it's best to be professional and let it go. After a couple of days, if you're not reliant on them financially, you won't even give them a second thought.

Freelance job Platforms

There are many online freelancer platforms, where you advertise your services and clients 'hire' you, places like People Per Hour (PPH), Upwork, et al, you may have heard of them, you may already be on them as a service provider. If you are, don't for one minute think this way of working is anything like being a business owner, it's not!

One thing you will notice about these sites is the cost for services is much lower than what you'll be charging. Why? Because a large majority of people on there are doing it alongside a full-time job, don't know their worth, think it'll get them clients who they can charge more to later on, or the people on there are from countries that don't have as high a cost of living as we do. It's also full of potential clients who want things done as cheaply as possible, and there will always be people like that, you don't need them.

Even if you use the platform for 'experience' you're taking work away from a virtual assistant trying to make a living. You don't need experience, because you're only offering services you're good at remember. And, if you're really stuck on 'getting experience' you can do it ethically and not by devaluing yourself.

I've never met anyone who has succeeded with PPH, etc. I've read comments online from people who say they have, but, we all know to take those with a pinch of salt, don't we? It's like those pictures of friends online in their idyllic relationships who, in reality, hate each other.

These sites are demoralising, it'll set you back, knock your confidence and bring in elements of self-doubt. You don't need that, you need to focus on your new adventure and put your energy there.

Must Haves

Again, this list is by no means an exhaustive one and there will be people throughout your journey who advise you on other must haves. These are just some of the essentials I've invested in to help me run my business safely and efficiently.

- **Insurance** – I removed a 'bad client' early on in my business, she was a big money earner for me, but she'd turned into the devil client. She was completely IT illiterate and had no real plan or goal for her business. She was chaotic. One minute she'd phone or email and say; *'I need this done urgently'.* I would do it, then I'd get *'I now need it done this way, urgently'.* Obviously, it was her money going down the drain, but I soon realised I can't work with chaotic people whose goals constantly change, it's stressful and not for me. Anyway, she didn't like being dumped and her lack of IT skills meant she didn't understand how documents were stored on the cloud, despite many explanatory emails, a video and a screen share via Skype. She could see the documents were created by me and was convinced they were therefore owned by me. But they were in her drive, one I no longer had access to, because I'd removed my access when I ceased our working relationship. She just couldn't understand and, as always, wouldn't listen.

  The next thing I knew there was a recorded delivery solicitors letter addressed to me saying she would take legal action if I didn't give her back her files. Luckily the solicitor understood how cloud storage worked and she went away, but it cost her £1800. It cost me a couple of hours and a few more in stress, explaining myself, but it could've got ugly and possibly expensive if she'd kept on. I was confident in what I was saying and reassured that I had insurance to back me up should it continue to be a stressful mess.

- **Back-up** – All my documents are saved on the cloud, using Google Drive or Dropbox, nothing is saved on my desktop that can't be lost. That way I can access the documents at any time, using any device. I just need to remember my passwords. There's also something in my office which the boyfriend installed, it backs everything up and I am not allowed to ever turn it off AGAIN! Get into the habit of saving everything on the cloud, whether you use Dropbox, Office 365, Google Drive or something else.

- **Accounting system** – Whether you use an online system, like FreeAgent, or use Excel, make sure you have something ready for keeping on top of your accounts. Diarise time to update it monthly (go on, do it now, you'll thank me for it!) and keep all your receipts in one place. When it gets to the end of your first year you'll be gutted if you have to waste endless time getting everything in order, remembering what you bought and why, whether it was even business related. I usually take invoicing day off to reward myself for a month of hard work.

- **Spare laptop** – Before I bought my MAC I had a cheap (under £200) laptop. It soon became an absolute nightmare once I'd installed a couple of programmes on it, but I've kept it as my back up. I firmly believe this is essential, as we no longer have an IT team to help us out when something goes wrong. This back up will be invaluable should anything happen to your usual device. It's also further proof that you should avoid saving anything to the desktop.

- **Spare phone** – Mine met with a pavement one day and was rendered absolutely useless, aided by me punching it to turn a call off that I was on at the time. I bought myself a very cheap mobile while I sourced a replacement smartphone. It was under £15 and simply makes and receives calls and texts, nothing else. It now sits in a drawer ready for the next time I have butter fingers.

- **Reliable hosting** – Your website will be the go to place for many potential clients before they get in touch with you, if yours isn't working they will go to the next one on Google and probably won't bother coming back. Check your site regularly and ensure you have hosts who can get you back online within a few hours should anything go wrong. My hosts respond to my queries 24/7 and in plain English. Yours should too.

- **Reliable internet** – Obviously essential, but sometimes out of your control, which is why I recommend you have…

- **Access to a dongle** – I've got one I can top up as and when I need it, with no monthly subscription, to use in cafés, on trains or when my neighbour decides to reverse into the internet exchange box in our street! It's safer, more reliable and another essential back up for when your home Wi-Fi goes down, which it will.

- **List of cafés and drop-in co-working places with Wi-Fi!** - I recommend you take headphones if you've been working alone for a while as the sudden noise is deafening and distracting. You could also use a local library or there may be co-working places in your area that allow you to drop in. Research places in advance that you can use before the worst-case scenario happens. This will also be great local knowledge to share with local clients. I also find this useful if the water or electricity ever goes off in the area.

And, as you get busier seek out a couple of virtual assistants you can rely on and call upon to help you should you need to outsource any tasks if things go upside down, or if you get sick.

Losing Clients
(how to prepare and avoid)

It'll happen, sometimes it'll be their choice and sometimes it'll be yours and sometimes it may come out of the blue! It's no different to being employed and your employers saying; 'we're just going to have a reshuffle, there won't be any redundancies, we promise'. Next thing you know you've got a calendar invite for a 'job fair'. No job is for life, and the same goes for being your own boss, external influences can often floor the most successful businessman/woman. So, don't worry about losing clients, it's not necessarily a reflection of you. There's lots you can do to protect yourself from it making too much of an impact.

My number one tip to protect yourself is, never rely on one client to pay your bills! This is so important. As I mentioned previously, I make sure no one client takes up more than 20% of the time I need to work to survive financially.

But why shouldn't you? Simple answer lies in the question; *what if they suddenly decide they don't need you anymore?*

It's well documented that the self-employed have far fewer employment rights and more financial risk than employees, but for many small business owners that's exactly why they'll choose to work with you - we're less hassle, no real commitment and we offer enormous flexibility to work with us as and when the need arises.

If your client doesn't need you anymore; whether that be because they do not have the capital to pay you or no longer have any work for you, then they can stop working with you more or less when they choose.

It's therefore, our responsibility to ensure we're not reliant on just one client, and here's some ideas how:

Keep on everyone's radar

Always keep on top of your online and / or face to face presence, however you have found clients previously, keep doing it, maybe to a slightly lesser degree if you're flat out, but don't stop. While you're not 'networking' someone else will be!

Respond to enquiries

I'd been trying to get a carpenter to alter two internal doors for around 2 months. You'd think I was asking someone to come out and build the ark, while blindfolded and with only their finger nails as tools for all the response I had.

I'd contacted eight and only one responded, then at the eleventh hour he texted to say he was *'stuck on another job'*. Clearly, he thought I'd just arrived on the aforementioned ark.

I would not recommend any of them and people won't recommend you in the future if you don't reply to enquiries. Build email time into every day, including checking your spam folder.

I check my spam folder twice a day, every day.

Just this year I almost missed out on two enquiries, Bitcoin and some mystery inheritance from a dead aunt I didn't know I had in a third world country.

Bad Clients

You'll get them, but it's fine. There are difficult people in all walks of life. It's how you deal with them that matters, how you *don't* let them affect you.

You can either deal with them yourself and put an end to the way things are making you feel or, much like a game of Monopoly, just wait for someone to walk off in a massive huff.

Your work life doesn't have to be controlled by anyone else anymore, you're free to decide what pulls and pushes there are on your time. But, you will come against people who are difficult and challenging and there will be some conflicts along the way. We'll call these people 'difficult'.

A couple of traits I've attributed to *'difficult'* clients are listed below. These are just my opinion, you may relish working for such people, but that's the beauty, you get to choose:

Micro managers; if someone has set you a clear task, with a deadline, they don't need to be asking you every few emails how far you've got, have you done this, etc. It's terribly frustrating and if they're on an hourly rate it's costing them extra money. Remind them it would probably be more cost effective if they just let you get on, that should keep them quiet.

Control freaks; they'll set a task, you complete it exactly to their brief then they want to change one little bit, every bloody time, so they can say 'that's my work'. It's frustrating and takes up your time, this is why you should always overestimate the time a project or task will take you, to cater for this kind of client.

Bad payers; once is noticeable, twice is a habit. Never, ever let anyone get away with not paying you. You're not the bigger person walking away from it, that's ridiculous behaviour and you'll be walked over again and again. Deal with it, let that person know they've had your time and your time is money. Keep on, ask politely the first time and then add interest. I ask for 75% up front from new clients as I was almost stung in my first few months by a convicted fraudster. I got my money because I didn't let it go, many small businesses didn't because they gave up. He owes hundreds of thousands of pounds, so I was wise to be tenacious. A good way to avoid two months of non-payment is to set your payment terms to seven days. That way, you're not a whole two months down the line before you can chase them.

Over friendly; I had one client who became over friendly, trying to become a friend and it put me into a position where I was willing to bend over backwards for them. Never again.

Urgency; their lack of planning is not your problem and you're not at a client's beck and call, unless they're willing to pay more for it. It's okay sometimes to be a hero, but make sure it doesn't become a habit or ruin your love for what you're doing.

---

*Don't forget you work **with** each other, learn to stop yourself saying you work for 'X'. Yes, you make their life easier and do the tasks they often don't enjoy, but you're equals.
You're just as brilliant. They don't own you!*

You'll want to do your very best for your clients at all times, however they can sometimes perceive that as not being enough or get used to you going above and beyond and take it for granted. As an example, on a couple of occasions I travelled to see a client in a local town. It'd be a whole day spent out of the office and I wouldn't charge anything, I thought it was good for building relationships. I'd come away with a list of tasks to do, so that was cool. However, I noticed that over the next week or so they'd start emailing and say; *I don't need you to do that now*' or *'I've done that'* and the list of tasks would dwindle to very little. I also used to work some weekends for this particular client at no extra charge! I know, I know, but I did say we all make mistakes. I've learnt from it.

Slowly she started to turn into a nightmare client, with vague requests for tasks, cancelling tasks that she'd previously requested, it got to the point where little would be right, because she wasn't communicating properly. My confidence got knocked slightly and I was no longer enjoying working for her, but I wanted to see her through a potentially busy period (and weekend work) before I made my excuses.

You may well be nodding here. You know the sort of person in an office, they only notice when you're late for work, never the instances where you've got there early. This is when they start taking you for granted.

My only mistake here was being efficient and going above and beyond, so I now charge extra for weekend work and I charge travel and meeting time when a client wants a face to face meeting, it'll stop me feeling aggrieved if they turn into a bad client.

I got rid and as usual, it made room for new more exciting clients really quickly as I'd kept my marketing going. You'll find that happens, when one door closes so many others open.

Clients will let you down, just like you will let them down, but if you're sure you've always done your very best and met the criteria of the task then it's probably their problem and not yours. You never really know what's going on in someone's life; money problems, marriage problems and you may well never know, so bury it early on and use that energy to replace them. You don't need negative people, life is short, this is your life. Only surround yourself with people who enhance your life not take away from it.

It's important to try and maintain a cordial professional relationship, so if things go wrong or you have a concern you can address it. You're not best friends, you're business associates.

Your client's reputation is just as important as yours, so if things start grating on you, step back and share everything with a relative or friend you can trust to give you honest advice and who can judge if you're being over sensitive, unprofessional or difficult, or if it's the client and the time has come to have a word or replace them.

Avoid replying to emails immediately, or in the heat of the moment, it's hard but you'll thank yourself after a night's sleep.

Use the energy to find another client to replace them, because if their conflicting behaviour continues you're probably not going to want to carry on working with them anyway. Of course, if you've followed the 20% rule meaning you are not reliant on one client then you can get rid of them when you've had enough.

Plus, you never know when they might need you again or you might need them, so walk away and say as little as possible to upset them.

Money is often at the root of personality change in business, but you may never know the real reason, so give it no extra thought.

In fact, that's this chapter over. Let's move on.

What Should you Charge?

Is this the chapter you've been looking forward to the most? I wish I could see your face when you know what you're going to be charging. Let's go...

Firstly, to get into the right mindset, we're going to try and stop referring to it as your hourly rate, instead we'll call it your hourly worth.

If you haven't already; Google a few virtual assistants in your area and let's look at their hourly rate. I'm guessing it's going to be anything from £25 to £40 an hour. So, let's set your rate at £15 so you get the clients, yeah? No!

Rule number one, don't undercut your competition. You don't want to make enemies before your business name has even dried on the page. Plus, charging less... you've got it... devalues you and our industry, which is why we're calling it your hourly worth. You're not worth less than anyone else, are you?

If you're wondering whether or not virtual assistants actually get paid between £25 and £40 the answer is yes, yes we do.

So, let's start at £25 and work our way up.

Go and grab, or download, three months of recent bank statements:

- Highlight all regular outgoings* in one colour

- Highlight any regular income, excluding wages, in another (i.e. child benefit, child support, pension, etc.)

For this exercise I'll use the following figures:

Outgoings: £1,100

Income (when not employed): £0

So, you need to earn at least £1100 a month.

£1,100 x 12 months = £13,200 per annum

£13,200 divided by 52 weeks = £254 a week

Let's start you working at 25 hours a week as a virtual assistant.

25 hours x £25 = £625 a week! You're quids in already (always put away 30% of your income ready for your tax bill – but always double check this in case there have been any changes between me writing this and you reading it.)

Obviously, you're not going to achieve 25 hours a week overnight, so the minimum you need to work at £25 an hour would be £254 divided by £25 = 10 hours.

Or, start at £30 and it looks even better; £254 divided by £30 = 8.5 hours.

Your location is irrelevant, you work virtually so you can access clients all over the country.

And before you ask, yes, you're worth that.

Still not 100% convinced?

Someone once said to me: *'When someone tells you you're too expensive, add 'for me' silently to the end of their sentence. You're too expensive *for them*'.* This may help change any elements of self-doubt that creep in when people want to 'haggle'.

Remember, don't undercut your competition or we can't be friends.

I can't stress this enough, hence why I keep banging on about it. You've only got me nagging at you in this book, imagine how my poor boyfriend feels day in day out! If you undercut other virtual assistants you'll weaken and devalue the virtual assistant industry. You'll alienate other people and create enemies. Competition is not the enemy, in fact your competitors could become great business associates.

Now you've set your fee and you've accepted you're worth it, you may be challenged to remember it from time to time. It'll be ever so tempting to accept a new client at a reduced rate just to get the client. I get that, but don't, and here's why:

If you work for 20% less for a client, that's 20% more work you have to do every hour.

If you reduce your fee, you'll have to work more hours. If you need £150 a day, charging £30 an hour you only need to work five hours. If you lower your hourly rate you'll have to work more hours, ask yourself in what circumstances and for whom you're willing to do that? No one I hope. Why would you want to sacrifice your time because someone wants to walk all over you and devalue you? If you can think of someone, pop it on your noticeboard, but first let's talk about charities.

I support one charity, by donating money monthly, but no one gets my time for free. Charities and start-up businesses have to budget for admin!

Your fee should not be negotiable. It's set. It's not a guide price. You don't go to the supermarket and ask if you can have the weekly shop a bit cheaper because you've not budgeted right. Although I'd like to see you try it.

I once had a woman approach me to do some copy typing. She said she'd visited my website and then asked; *'what's your hourly rate?'* What that actually meant was, *'I saw your hourly rate, but can't afford you, is it negotiable?'*

I then, yeah this one you won't believe, I then had another enquiry from a lady who wanted some support in her business. Again, I was asked, *'what's your hourly rate?'*, and when I informed her she replied *'Oh, but it's a straightforward job so I thought you could do it for £9 an hour?'*. I kid you not! I don't care if I can do it with my eyes closed, if it's going to take an hour, it's my hourly rate, not just over a third of it.

So, practice saying no! It'll make you feel so good and then when you send your first invoice for your actual hourly worth you'll feel amazing.

If someone wants 15 hours every week on a retained basis, you might feel you can afford to discount as that's a great gig, but often those who want to pay less demand more, or perhaps it's a mindset thing and you feel like you don't want to give your all because they're getting you cheap? You'll also kick yourself if someone else comes along wanting five hours at full whack, because you may not have the time. So, set a limit before you open for business, for large jobs or retainers if you really want to.

Skill swaps. Yeah why not, if it's something you need and want. But ask whether you were going to buy it anyway or it saves you money. If it means you can't pay the mortgage that month, say no.

Discounts. People may wonder why – do you ever see an offer for an identical service or item below what everyone else is charging and wonder why? You should do! It can smack of a con, crap results, unprofessional or uncommitted.

Friends and family. I'd recommend not even giving a discount there, for the same reasons above. Do you want to work more hours just because they're a mate or a cousin? If yes, why? What's it getting you? Nothing, the client is benefiting and you're losing out. Don't say experience, you don't need it, you're already perfectly capable of carrying out the services you're offering, we covered that in the chapter 'what services should you offer?'.

Think of it this way too, if you usually only work five hours a day and drop your rate for someone, you're going to have to start working more hours a day to earn the difference.

This is a line I have used once before:

'I want every client to receive the same level of service, so I do not offer any discounts on my hourly rate.'

Introductory offers; why? How are you going to up your price at a later date? It's hard, trust me. I made that mistake. Don't forget those introductory offers mean you'll have to work more hours, you'll undercut your mentors, undervalue the brand and there's no guarantee these clients will want to work with you at full whack.

I love two non-bio washing brands, but I have no allegiance to either, I'll just buy the one that's on offer. I don't think they're worth full price if they can sell them cheap. Is there anything you invest in only when it's on offer?

Exposure and Experience

'I've had three quotes at £9, £10 and £12, so I can't understand why you won't do it for around that price? The work is quite straight-forward and I will provide clear guidance.'

I've only had it twice, but it was twice in as many weeks and both potential clients thought it was justified because they could *'offer me exposure'.* I know, can you believe people actually use that line, while at the same time failing to understand why I wouldn't drop my hourly rate significantly because 'the work is quite straightforward'.

I also had one woman who wanted me to dedicate a couple of hours a week to her 'business' in exchange for shares in the company. The company was worth nothing, so she could've given me feathers, it would've been just as valuable.

I don't care if the work can be done with a pair of tights over my head and my hands behind my back, my hourly rate is still my hourly rate. An hour of my time is still the same no matter what the task. Exposure won't pay my household bills or support my child going through university, and and .... it doesn't help my charity shop addiction either!

People will promise you exposure on their 'really busy' websites or social media channels if you do something for free or for a reduced rate. You don't need it. It rarely brings in any good leads other than more people wanting stuff for free.

If a job is going to take you an hour then it's your hourly rate, END OF STORY.

Summary:

So, your hourly worth is: _____

» Minimum one hour work a month

» Everything is rounded up to the nearest half hour.

Chunks of time: _____

» Minimum 5 or 10 hours a month

Day rate: hourly rate x 10 (or more if this isn't going to cover your expenses, like fuel and food): _____

Associate hourly rate: _____ (we'll look at this a bit more in the 'associates' chapter, so you may want to leave this bit blank for now)

Don't forget to consider any future changes, for example interest rates increasing, child going to university, child benefit stopping, MOT's due, roof needs replacing, a big birthday.

For your own justification and to use promotionally, here's why working with a virtual assistant is still the better option for business owners:

☑ No long-term commitments

☑ No National Insurance

☑ No tax

☑ No holiday pay

☑ No pension

☑ No payroll expenses

☑ No extra accounting, just invoice in, pay it, jobs done

☑ No dramas!

TASK

Pop your hourly worth on your noticeboard and stick to it.
Promise?

Competitors

You may need to find a whole new mindset when you think about competitors. Big brands like a well-known supermarket will often market themselves by highlighting how much cheaper they are than other supermarkets, but as a small business owner although you're going to market yourself as the one to go to, it's not going to ever be a *'I'm better than that one because…'.*

Instead fellow virtual assistants may be one of your greatest leverages for success. You can learn from them, work with them and grow with them.

Identify a couple of local virtual assistants and send them an email to introduce yourself and say hello. After all, we're virtual so we're not chasing the same clients. This is what I sent to another local virtual assistant a few months after my business went live.

Hi,

I've been meaning to say hello since around March, but wasn't quite sure how to, so with a quiet day in the office there's no better time.

I just wanted to introduce myself; you may have seen me floating about, so it's rude of me not to have been in touch sooner. I've started my own virtual assistant one-man band business in Swindon, working in the corporate world wasn't very good for stress levels, so I thought I would try it on my own so I can manage my days and my stress levels better.

Anyway, I am in awe of your success and I really hope we might get an opportunity to have a coffee one day so I can say hello properly. Will you be at the South West Expo on the 30th?

It'll be great to hear from you,

Catherine

What followed was an invite to her office and a chat about how her business had grown over four years, plus a surprise…

Hi Catherine,

I wanted to get in touch also, we went to school together.

Congratulations on starting your own business, it's a big step so I applaud all that do so.

It would be great to catch up and I'll also be at the Business Show but if you fancy meeting up beforehand let me know, you're more than welcome to pop into the office and say hi.

I hadn't realised that we'd been at school together as she had a new surname. We'd also worked for the same employer at 16, a large international company, she was a secretary, a very good secretary and a lovely person, so it wasn't a surprise she was now running a successful virtual assistant business.

When we met it was apparent her services were quite different to mine. She offered call handling, payroll and more document-based work, so it was great to meet her to get an understanding of her area of expertise and she mine, so we could recommend each other to clients who wanted services we didn't offer, and we have on a few occasions.

Reasons to get in touch:

- ☑ Make a friend in the same sector
- ☑ Share workload
- ☑ Become associates
- ☑ Learn from each other
- ☑ Share resources

Don't emulate any other virtual assistants, we're all different and it'll soon get noticed if you're copying others. A couple of virtual assistants I'm friendly with have noticed people copying our social media and website content from time to time, it's slightly awkward for them when you have to call them out on it and with everything online having a date, it's not hard to prove who published something first. Stand out for being unique.

And, as I mention in the chapter 'things to avoid', copying isn't acceptable in any form.

As you become successful and other virtual assistants start to introduce themselves to you, be as genuinely welcoming as you'd have wanted. Absolutely, become acquaintances, you may wish to use them as associates, but don't spend time coaching them, you're not their free learning platform, so keep your wits about you and some cards close to your chest. I had a client's daughter contact me on LinkedIn once saying she'd like to connect because she wanted to learn to be a virtual assistant. Oh right, so you want to learn from me and then take over your Dad's admin? Not happening on my watch.

Associates
(you and them)

You

Some virtual assistants start off as self-employed associates to other established virtual assistants, it could be a great way to get experience of running a business and ease yourself into being a business owner.

As an associate, you'd usually command a lower hourly rate than the virtual assistant you're working with, this is because they've sourced the client, done the marketing, liaised with the client and are having to spend time communicating the work to you.

The virtual assistant may also ask you to sign a non-disclosure agreement (NDA), which will probably primarily be to prevent you contacting the client you're doing the work for directly, as well as other confidentiality clauses.

Before we talk about rates, the same thing applies as with your hourly rate, don't undervalue yourself, don't undercut others and don't see this as 'experience', you already know how to do the tasks, you're just easing yourself into being a business owner. Go in too cheap and people may question your ability to do a task.

I'd like to suggest not going below 20% of your hourly rate, so if the virtual assistant you're working with charges the same hourly rate as you, e.g. £25 an hour, you could start negotiations at £22.50 (10% your usual hourly rate) and have a lower limit of £20 (20%). You will need to think about your associate rate minimum before the conversation comes up, so you're ready on your feet.

If you do any associate work you could get a testimonial or recommendation afterwards from the virtual assistant you worked with, or better still, from the client you did the work for, if the virtual assistant you're associate to is happy with that.

Them

Another reason it's a good idea to build relationships with fellow virtual assistants is so you can identify potential associates for you to outsource to in the event of an emergency, poorly child, poorly animal, holidays, essential waxing, VA flu or if you're at capacity.

> *I've outsourced a couple of times on big projects with a short deadline but have always let the client know from the start, not for their permission, but for data protection purposes more than anything.*

I only ever outsource if I am 100% confident the virtual assistant can deliver to the same standard as me, because it's my reputation on the line and if they do a bad job I'd have to do it again, leaving me out of pocket.

Some virtual assistants outsource tasks they **don't want to do**, like taking phone calls. The virtual assistant pays the call handling company and then charges the client a bit more to make a profit. This is sometimes called passive income, because you're earning money while doing very little.

Others outsource tasks they **can't do**, which I am not comfortable doing. I only ever outsource tasks I am confident doing myself otherwise how would I know they've been done correctly?

Tips for engaging an associate virtual assistant:

» Make sure your instructions are clear and to the clients brief so you don't have to spend any extra time tidying up the task when it comes back from your associate.

» I'd also recommend you ask them to sign a non-disclosure agreement so that the information they're privy to isn't shared and so they don't contact the client directly. If the client has given you an NDA to sign, they may want the associate to sign it too.

Marketing Your Business

Marketing: '*The action or business of promoting and selling products or services.*'

I am not a marketer but have worked with some great marketers and have learned to successfully market myself and my business to bring me a stable income. Here I'll share what's worked for me and hopefully these tips will start you off and sustain you throughout your marketing journey to a successful business.

This is an area of your business, unless you have a background in marketing, that will sometimes be trial and error, so don't worry about pulling in a paying crowd with every attempt.

You'll find that in much of this chapter I pose questions, which is what you'll be doing yourself with your marketing. Putting yourself in your audience's shoes and questioning what you're delivering to them.

This is also where business groups, LinkedIn and pages on Facebook will be beneficial, you can watch and see how others are promoting themselves, see what works for them and see what marketing you enjoy reading. Even consider the bigger national brands that you invest in.

Study their approach, write down their consistencies, and how it makes you feel;

> » Can you identify their audience from the marketing – how?
>
> » Would you buy from them? Why?

Find a brand you wouldn't buy from and again ask yourself why;

- » Is it their ethos?
- » Is it because you're not their target market?

Think about make-up, why do you buy some brands over others?

- » How did you first hear about the brand?
- » Is it to do with any aspects of their marketing?

Don't get too hung up on immediate responses, likes or comments on your posts, sometimes people are watching but not interacting. A week before I started writing this book I received a call from a new client who said; *'I keep looking at your website, in fact I've been looking for three months and have just found the time to call'.*

Another of my clients read a few of my blogs on my website before he phoned me and now we work together every month. If it wasn't for my Google analytics I'd never have known anyone was looking at my blog at all.

'Do, analyse, adapt', is the motto I've adopted.

TASK

Earlier we looked at what services you might offer, take that list and think about why? What problems are you solving? What are your clients pain points? This is how you'll start targeting your marketing.

Those notes can then be turned into social media posts, text for a blog, text on your website or answers to questions at networking events.

How Much to Share?

I was lucky enough to undertake an in-house 'tone of voice' course when I worked at the National Trust, as they worked to adapt their tone of voice from instructional to encouraging thought. i.e. *'You're going the wrong way! Keep off the land, it upsets the sheep'* was turned into *'sheep graze here regularly and aren't always welcoming of humans. There's another path just 500 yards to your right, which we think you'll enjoy much more'.* Tone of voice is so important, and now the world welcomes a genuine, slightly informal tone, unless you're a government minister – but they could learn a thing or two in my opinion.

How would it make you feel if you'd decided to donate lots of bits and pieces to a charity shop, and on arrival found they were closed with a sign on the door saying;

'Don't drop charity donations in the door way!'

Wouldn't it be better worded like this?

'Unfortunately, items left in the doorway often go missing. If you can, please return with your generous donation during opening hours.'

Be normal, talk conversationally. Imagine the best radio presenters, they make you feel like they're talking to you, not a million people, imagine your audience when you're writing a blog, email, social media post or doing your piece to camera in a video. Engage the listener, smile and practice those genuine eyes.

When I write articles for a client of mine I make it as conversational as possible. If the light is on in my office I worry to death a neighbour will see me pulling faces, laughing to myself and raising my eyebrows as my mind has the conversation with the audience.

TASK

Find some blogs on topics by various writers that interest you, maybe gardening, or summer holidays, and choose which ones engage you the most. Write down why, write down what you didn't enjoy. Was it too long? Was the heading misleading (clickbait)? Were there too many images? Not enough images? What was the tone?

Do this again with some blogs you didn't enjoy or couldn't even get started with and you'll find ways to enjoy writing them too.

Things to Avoid

Now you're a business owner you're not going to want the world seeing your drunken rants, family members making rude comments on your posts, or posts that reveal your personal beliefs, which could impact your business reputation. Yes, you can be exactly who you want to be and yes, I did say to be honest and genuine, but it's not necessary, or appropriate, for your clients, or potential clients to be involved in your personal life. Clients aren't your friends, they are business associates and I can guarantee there will be a time when one or more clients need to be managed out of your life, if they're 'friends' it can be much harder to disconnect.

Imagine if they owed you money yet you can see they're on holiday! Awkward.

My advice to myself has always been, never share what you wouldn't happily share with the Daily Mail! People can screenshot just about anything these days and they will! I do!

Now is as good a time as any to check your privacy settings on Facebook or anywhere else that's personal. Go on, I'll wait…

Calls to Action

As a reminder, a call to action is a directive or instruction to your audience to perform your desired instruction.

You'll see and hear calls to action all the time, without giving them a second thought. It's how marketers get us to buy stuff and how people get us to do things with or for them. A text message from a friend; *'Okay, see you at the pub at 8pm'.* The call to action is for you to be at the pub at 8pm.

Teachers speak to the class then ask the class to confirm their learning by performing a task *'write a 1,000-word essay', 'get into groups and make a model'* or the call to action to me was usually *'go and stand outside the classroom'.*

Another example you'll have noticed is when a TV channel is advertising a new series it wants you to watch, they'll prompt you to record it or set a reminder, this is their call to action to you.

Thinking about some TV adverts you may have seen recently. Maybe they included the company's website address at the end of the ad, or the narrator saying, 'visit us on the high street in town'.

You don't always need to add a call to action but try and work it into your posts to ensure your audience are directed to what you have to offer (whether it's tips or services) as often as possible, without being too pushy.

And the best bit, you get to choose where you want the audience to go, what your call to action is going to be. I prefer emails over telephone calls, for various reasons, but mainly telephones calls are a zap on time, whereas emails are easier and more to the point, plus I can answer them when I am free, not while I am working on another client's tasks, so I tend to use my email or web address as my call to action, wherever I want the reader to go.

Example:

If I do a post about bookkeeping my call to action would either be for the reader to email me, depending on the content, or a link to my bookkeeping service and rates.

Here's some examples of using different calls to action:

'Did you know you can add interest to unpaid invoices? In fact, it's encouraged by the UK government. If you have unpaid invoices and want to know what you can claim in interest check out the gov.uk website: www.gov.uk'

I'm just giving a tip here and showing my knowledge and proving what I say with backed up evidence.

'Do you have unpaid invoices? If so, get in touch and we can work out what interest you can add to them. Don't let them go, you worked hard for your money! (my email address)'

Here I am offering a service addressing a client's pain point with a quick call to action as to how they can proceed if they want to work with me.

'Bookkeeping, an essential part of your business, but for many a real chore and a time-sucking task. Whereas, I love it and more importantly, it gives my clients time to spend on their business. (link to my bookkeeping services)'

A direct boom! Offering my service, identifying it as a pain point for many and letting them know I can do it for them. Linking them to my rates page stops the time wasters calling or emailing and asking *'how much?'*

I always add a call to action to each of my blog posts, whether it's a link to another relevant blog post, a link to my services or to one of my social media pages. It's wherever I want the reader to go.

Tip: *If you are including a link to an external page on your website (such as a government website) be sure that the link opens in a new window/tab rather than taking the reader away from your website. This can be set when you insert the url.*

What will be your calls to action? Where do you want people to ultimately end up? Where would you want to end up if you were the client?

Would you want the option to get in touch by email, to read more, to check the rates, to call?

Avoid being too vague or salesy, people don't have time for games, especially not in today's fast-paced world.

For example, avoid things like:

'Call me to find out how I can make life easier for you'

Instead try;

'I work with clients to help make their lives easier, by managing their diaries, their paperwork, bookkeeping. To find out more about how I might be able to help you, take a look at my website, (www.delegateva.co.uk)'.

Equally, allow people to browse. Think about how you feel in a shop if someone keeps coming up asking if you need help, or if you're on a website and a pop up keeps asking you to fill in a survey?

TASK

Think about how you'd like your potential clients to get in touch with you.

If you've already written some blog posts or LinkedIn articles do they include a call to action? If not, add one in to them now.

Write down your various calls to action and pop them on your noticeboard, so you don't forget to add them.

Consistency

Having a consistent presence is key.

Marketing through the ages has changed significantly, and as far as I can see, will continue to do so. We used to sell things by placing a free black and white ad in a local paper, no images, just a little bit of text and a home phone number. Now we can reach the whole world with colour, images and a phone number you can be contacted on wherever you are at any given moment. It's the same for your business, you can reach the world.

You'll always find someone who hates what you love, so keep that in mind when sharing tips, especially if you fear giving away too much. You're not trying to convert them to your way of thinking, you're trying to make them understand that you can do what they don't enjoy doing. Can you believe there are people out there who don't like admin! I know, strange.

Be inspired by the posts, blogs and articles of others. You may find some fantastic articles online that your audience will love, if you share them it'll no doubt be useful for them, but don't forget it takes them away from you! Can you perhaps re-write the blog, putting your own experiences and insight into it? But, don't copy it! That's uncool and illegal.

Non-stop marketing

Have you ever seen a Twitter account where the last tweet was months, or years ago? It makes me wonder whether they're still in business. Does it you? It's likely the platform just isn't working for them and they've given up bothering, or they're too busy to spend any time thinking of content to post. Epic fail!

Keep marketing even when you're busy, so you don't suddenly need to ramp it up when you lose a client. If you've let it slip it could take a good while to get back in to it and engage your audience, learn what's new, what works etc., causing you extra stress, extra time and more money. Remember, your time is money!

Summary:

> »   Being a reliable, efficient virtual assistant is an achievable business option, so be persistent, consistent and strong.

Social Media

Social media is huge, as I know you'll be aware.

Like it or loathe it, it's going to become a huge part of your life if you're going to get in front of people regularly and to an extent, for free, i.e. you don't need to spend any money, but your time is money remember, so try and ration yourself.

You're definitely going to need a Facebook business page (I currently make most of my business contacts via Facebook) and a relevant up-to-date LinkedIn profile. I appreciate this might be difficult to do if you're still employed but see what your human resources department says. Twitter, it's up to you, maybe look at that at a later date as currently I find Twitter rather busy and lacking a little direction. Instagram, by all means, but you're going to need to be consistent and regular on them all. Can you manage multiple accounts when you're at capacity?

As I mentioned, if I ever visit a business page on social media and notice there have been no posts or interaction for months I assume *'out of business'* or if they're a small business; *'too busy, I won't contact'*.

We've all seen the adverts on the television advising the vulnerable to be careful and mindful of who they're talking to online, it's going to be a similar experience for you too as a business owner, but more around listening. Use the platforms to learn, watch how others do things well, but, like I said previously, be mindful that sometimes everyone's an 'expert' of everything. Follow up what you learn online by reading further publications and articles, ideally from trusted sources or the horse's mouth.

Always check facts before running away with them, sharing them and telling others because it will do your credibility the world of good if you're seen as someone who only shares facts.

Here's some more tips on starting or maintaining your social media presence, which I had published in a local business magazine:

Where do I find my audience?

Invite your friends to like your social media pages, and connect with past colleagues, acquaintances on LinkedIn. You really never know who these people might know or when they might need your product or service themselves.

First or third person? Us or me?

Personally, I prefer honesty. Why say 'us' if it's only 'you' in the business? It makes me rather suspicious when people talk about 'us' when it's just them in their spare room office. I know it was the norm once, but currently, it's rather on trend to be a one-man band.

Consider this; do you only invest in services (e.g. plumbers, hairdressers) based on how many people run the company or, is buying from someone you can trust more important?

Tone of voice

These days it's all very casual and natural. You can drop the 'yourself' and 'myself' and be much more conversational with people. Everyone's time is so limited, they just want you to get to the point. Write as you would speak, so you also attract people who will get you, you'll more likely enjoy working with each other then as well.

Address your post as if you're talking to one person or a small audience, that way it feels personal for the reader and makes it easier for them to respond.

Which platforms shall I use?

That's up to you. You may want to start with all of them but be realistic. As a service provider you'll possibly struggle to think of engaging regular content for Pinterest or Instagram, so maybe leave those for a later date. Facebook is my go to platform and where I have 'met' almost all of my clients. It's certainly very active, but things do change. Facebook after all is a social interaction platform, so don't rely on it as your only means of marketing. Things will and do change.

How many followers do I need to be successful?

One! If that 'one' is your ideal customer and they're willing to pay you double what you need to survive every month for the next 20 years, then you really only need one follower. However, that's unlikely. But my point is; you don't need X amount of followers to be noticed or successful, you just need to engage your audience with relevant quality content.

How often shall I post?

I think you should only post when you have something to say, and if you don't have anything to say then you can break the silence by sharing useful content from other people, or from media sources, but don't worry about saying something every day. Start off once or twice a week perhaps and add to it when there's something to say or share. As you're able to schedule posts you don't have to get everything out at once. Spread it out.

When you're busy make sure you're still as active on your social channels as you always were by scheduling content or by outsourcing. Whatever you choose you need to stay in people's minds or your competitors will!

When will I make my millions?*

Patience. As above, be consistent and let your audience know you're there for the long haul. Not everyone likes or comments on posts, many people will be watching, learning and remembering you / your business and will be in touch in their own time. Just keep at it and never underestimate the power of social media.

Reflect

After 3-6 months reflect on what you've done. Take advantage of the free insights available on your chosen platforms, and Google Analytics, and analyse:

- » What content was received well?

- » What times of day were posts better received?

- » What didn't work so well? Why?

- » What can you do differently?

- » Are all platforms 'working' for me?

Everything may be going well, or you may want to re-consider how you're 'doing social media'.

Don't give up, it's a fabulous, virtually free, way to market you and your business.

There are some great books and social media planners out there to kick-start or improve your social media, but for now go and have some fun with it. I still do now.

*you may not make millions, but if you do – remember me!

Social media content planner

Date	Twitter	Facebook	LinkedIn	Instagram
1st January	This is where you'll pop your content so you can return at a later date to see what you posted, with ease and copy and paste it again if needs be.			
2nd January			Or you could just pop in reminders for yourself, e.g, Post link to blog post on time management	
3rd January				
4th January				
5th January				
6th January				
7th January				
8th January				
9th January	Wish Catherine a happy birthday!	Wish Catherine a happy birthday!	Wish Catherine a happy birthday!	

There's a free social media planner example on the website, www. howtobeava.co.uk - download it if you haven't already.

Things to Avoid

Mistakes happen, end of chapter...

No seriously, they do. You'll make mistakes on client work and in your own business, life is trial and error much of the time and so too in business. There's not, at time of writing, a handbook on how to live life, because everyone's life is different, but there are guidance notes for just about everything and the same goes for running a business.

I'm going to list a few things that I see some virtual assistants and other small business owners do, which I don't think work in today's market and may hold back your progress:

- **Saying yes to something you can't do.** I get a lot of enquiries from business owners who have used a virtual assistant for a task and they've really messed it up or started it and then gone awol. This is always down to them accepting a task they've never done before, not telling the client and panicking. As I said earlier, be honest. It's less stress for everyone in the long run.

- **Talking in the third person.** Who do you think is going to read text written in that way and consider someone else has written it for them? They're going to know it's you and then it sounds daft, doesn't it? The only thing that should be written in the third person should be testimonials and recommendations.

- **Us or I?** Here I go again. This is really your choice, but you're about to start building your reputation. I'd recommend avoiding saying we or us if it's just you, regardless of whether you intend to grow in the future. Be honest and up front from the start. So many people run their businesses alone, you no longer have to give any impression other than the truth. Also, if you give the impression you're a large team then your client might wonder whether he'll get a consistent service and be able to dip in and out of working with you, or whether he'll have to re-explain himself every time he needs a task done.

- **Talking to the whole world.** As I mentioned earlier, define an audience and speak to them as if they're the only one you're talking to. Make it too general and it's just white noise in a crowded room. Identify, agitate, solve. You really can't sell to everyone, it's impossible, so pick on certain areas and hit them with your stuff.

- **Trying too hard.** I've seen virtual assistants suck up like there's no tomorrow, you're an equal business owner. Be grateful graciously.

- **Being unprofessional.** Be yourself, but always consider that what goes online, stays online (or can be screen grabbed). I'm terrible for it. I am as blunt as blunt can be and very intolerant at times, so I give this advice without taking it myself. But I'm always happy to say everything I say online in person.

- **Using images without permission.** As in UK law, ignorance is not an excuse. As a business owner you are responsible for ensuring you know what is right and wrong and that mate on Facebook is likely to be wrong. Also, just because you've seen everyone else doing it doesn't make it right.

'Sorry officer, I was speeding because that chap in the blue car was, so I thought if he can, I can?'

There are very strict, complicated licensing rules around using other people's images in any situation. In a nutshell, you can't just lift an image from Google and use it yourself, in any format. But of course, you're just a local virtual assistant with a following of 50 people, so who will notice anyway? Trust me, they will.

One of my clients recently used an image in one of their newsletters and within a few hours, yes hours, they had an email from the owner saying they were disappointed they'd not asked permission or credited them in anyway. They were lucky the owner chose that response and didn't just follow up with an invoice.

One virtual assistant posted in a group once that one of her clients had received a bill from the owner of an image she had used on his marketing; she 'had no idea you couldn't use images from Google'. The client had to pay way over £500! Ouch.

There are *lots of websites* out there that offer license free images, my favourite being Canva which I explain a little more about in the 'Useful websites' section at the end of this book.

- **Plagiarism:** The stealing and production of someone else's work, represented as your own. Just like images, you also can't use other people's content without their prior written permission, or by paying them royalties.

You don't have to be famous for someone to copy your content. I've had someone from Islamabad copy my summary on LinkedIn, when I confronted her she said, *'I've changed Swindon to Islamabad'*. Oh, that's okay then, not!

I've also had a virtual assistant copy text from my website, verbatim – she even forgot to change my business name to hers! I often find people who are using my content and it's often met with a 'how did you find out?'. Trust me, it's very easy.

Likewise, we can't copy anyone else's work. We can share it, and credit them, or link to where we found it, but we can't copy it and claim it as our own work. If in doubt, contact the author and ask for their written permission to share.

- **Bad grammar and spelling.** As I said at the beginning of this chapter, we all make mistakes. By the time you're reading this, this book would've been proofread and edited by a professional editor, paid for by me, but I can almost guarantee there will be at least one spelling or grammatical error in here, even the best people make mistakes. Don't be too methodical or you'll never get any content out there, but equally don't rush. You're not ever going to be breaking news first, so take your time, step away from your finished content return later and read through it again, you'll be more likely to find any glaring mistakes.

  If you know you're not too hot on spelling and grammar you can use programmes to check things through for you, I use Grammarly sometimes, which integrates with other programmes like Gmail, Facebook, Twitter, Hootsuite, LinkedIn, etc and helps me avoid too many sloppy mistakes.

  I also have my daughter who sends me screenshots of any offending posts along with the correction marked with an asterisk! She's available on request!

Of course, the list isn't exhaustive and it's always how you deal with things afterwards that really matter. I see mistakes as a learning experience, unless I keep doing them then it's embarrassing.

Without mistakes I'd probably walk around with my nose in the air thinking I'm the bee's knees, so personally, I like making them, occasionally.

Useful Websites

Gmail

My favourite. It's so intuitive and it's free up to a certain gigabyte, which you'll be hard pushed to reach. Having a Gmail account also gives you access to Google Drive, a cloud -based platform for storing all documents and images. Google Drive can also be shared with your clients, so you can co-work on documents. In addition, as everything is saved online the latest version of any file is accessible from any device (even your phone) as they sync.

Dropbox.com

Dropbox is another cloud-based platform for storing documents and images, which you can then share and collaborate with anyone you choose to. I use this in addition to Google Drive as some of my clients prefer sharing in this way.

WeTransfer.com

This is a great free tool for sharing large documents with anyone who has an email address. One to bookmark for when the need arises.

Toggl.com

Toggl is a time recording system which is free to use, there is a paid option for when your business gets bigger, but at the beginning you won't need to invest in that. Toggl will become a huge part of every working day for you. You can stop and start the clock every time you're working on a client's tasks, so you know exactly how long things are taking. You can also run reports to see how much time you've spent on a client's tasks and share that with them as often as you / they want and attach them to your invoices. It's an invaluable tool.

LastPass.com

How many passwords? You'll also be storing passwords for client's accounts too in time, so you really can't be expected to remember everything and writing them down in the back of a notebook isn't safe, secure or wise. Put simply and in their own words 'LastPass remembers all your passwords, so you don't have to'. Every time you visit a new website and set up a new account or input new login details LastPass automatically prompts you to save those details in its online vault, it then recalls them the next time you visit that website.

FreeAgent.com

This is one of the first things I invested in. FreeAgent feeds from your bank account to show all your transactions and enables you to match them to invoices and receipts. You can also record cash expenses and mileage expenses. You invoice directly from the program and can attach your time report from Toggl too enabling you to then match that invoice when the money is received. When you get to the point where you're sending out a few invoices a month this is a worthwhile investment. I saved 4-6 hours a month by investing in this, so it paid for itself immediately. I've also got a 10% off code, which I'm sure you'll love to use: 46dac370

Hootsuite.com

There are lots of platforms you can use to schedule content to various social media channels, but this is my platform of choice. Again, you can use the free version for up to a maximum number of accounts and then you can move onto their price plan if you want / need to add more.

Canva.com

Oh my God! This is amazing for creating memes, social media images, website and blog images, etc. It's so addictive. Again, you can use most of the functionality free of charge, but there are added features on the paid for version. I share my annual subscription with another virtual assistant.

Grammarly.com

Grammarly is a free online resource which helps to ensure your posts, documents and articles are mistake-free – but don't rely on it 100%, it seems to have off days. A paid for version of Grammarly is also available for greater support.

ecohosting.co.uk

This is something that must be right. If your website goes down an hour before you're posting a link to your fabulous new blog post which is directing everyone to your website you are not going to look too clever are you. You need hosts who will work with you, for you and in a timely non-jargon filled manner. For this I recommend ecohosting.

ICO.org.uk (Information Commissioners Office)

Here you'll find everything you need to know about data protection / General Data Protection Regulation (GDPR, previously known as Data Protection Act 1998).

Gov.uk

The UK Government website. For small business help and advice, including everything you need to know from HMRC.

Tfl.gov.uk

Tfl (Transport for London) in their own words; run the day-to-day operation of the capital's public transport network and manage London's main roads. This is a useful website for checking up-to-date travel information in the capital.

highways.gov.uk/traffic-information

Highways agency, here you'll find up to the minute information on road closures, accidents, etc.

nationalrail.co.uk

Up-to-date rail information for Great Britain. It's also always worth just checking the train operator's website too.

Packages to Learn

If you're not familiar with the following packages now will be a good time to take a look and familiarise yourself with them:

» Toggl – (FREE)

» Canva – (FREE)

» Hootsuite – (FREE)

» Google Drive – (FREE)

» DropBox - (FREE)

» LastPass – (FREE)

» Mailchimp – sign up for free and send newsletters to yourself until you know how to use it. Then, you can offer this as a service. You won't need to send newsletters to your clients, we're freeing up their time, not adding to it. (FREE.)

» WordPress – this is one that's worth an investment, as you can then offer updates and additions to client's websites as part of your service. WordPress is extremely popular at the moment, and many clients either don't have time or know how to make changes, so this really is invaluable. I've written a course to teach you how to Build and Maintain a WordPress website. Hop on over to the website to find out more. Once you've completed the course (it can be done in a weekend) you can then add WordPress maintenance as a service and stand out from the crowd! (INVESTMENT).

Summary of Terms

You'll come across so many different terms and you may well be familiar with all of the following, but just in case any are new to you, here are some that will crop up:

- **Call to action** (CTA) – a directive or instruction to your audience to perform your desired instruction. Don't forget to have a call to action in as many places as possible so your reader / audience can find out everything they need to know to start working with you.

- **Cloud** – this is where you'll be wanting to save client work, so you can all access it at any time.

- **Niche** – targeting your services or marketing to a small specific genre.

- **Non-disclosure agreement** (NDA) – clients or other virtual assistants may ask you to sign one of these to protect their intellectual property. It's fine to do so, but always read it through carefully in case there are any nonsense bits you're not happy with.

- **Sync** – you're going to want to make sure all your cloud-based programmes are always syncing in case your laptop / PC dies. Find out how to make sure it's working and regularly check.

- **Target audience** – who your marketing and promotional activity is aimed at. This is easier to identify when you know your niche.

- **Webinar** – You'll see lots of business owners / trainers doing webinars, and I do them regularly too. These are a great way to learn new stuff and are sometimes free. Great to watch / listen to while you're doing something else, if you can multi-task (I can't), or in the evening.

References

Page 25: SMART acronym. Dr. Doran (PhD) was a dedicated professor, author, entrepreneur and creator of the SMART acronym. Dr. Doran developed the SMART acronym in November 1981. Dr. Doran published a paper titled *'There's a S.M.A.R.T. Way to Write Management's Goals and Objectives.'*

Page 54: Virtual Assistant in the Flesh t-shirts were available from: www.virtualassistantshop.com

Page 63: YouTube: Richard Branson 'Fake it 'till you make it' on Twitter @ oscarmguti

What's Next?

I'll ask you again. If you were to write an autobiography how cool would it look to add a chapter 'successful business owner'? Go on, add it.

You've come this far, now it's time to put it all into practice and start your journey to become a successful virtual assistant, so don't let anything stand in your way (unless it's fizzy or covered in chocolate).

If you have any wobbles or need any support during your VA journey I offer Power Hours to anyone who is looking to set up as a VA or has already. I also run a membership for established virtual assistants – everything you need to know is here: www.howtobeava.co.uk.

Sometimes all we need is to know we are doing everything right.

I want to know how you're getting on, so let's connect if we haven't already:

Twitter: DelegateVA / howtobea_va

Facebook: DelegateVA / howtobeava

LinkedIn: DelegateVA

Instagram: DelegateVA / howtobea_va

About Me

I left school at 16 and went to college for about two weeks. I can't even remember what I was studying, but I didn't like it so I left and got my first job. It was local as an admin assistant for a national freight company and I loved it. I had far too much fun there, I worked hard but I was with a great team. I loved working on a computer, I loved organising paperwork and I loved having my own desk. I'd found my vocation.

Since then, for over 20 years, I have always worked in admin focused roles, apart from a stint as an IT night school lecturer teaching beginners and advanced IT courses at the local college. I've worked under the title of secretary, senior secretary, PA, director's executive assistant and as an admin manager, but I will be honest, the roles have never kept me busy for long as I work fast and efficiently. I love organising people, but equally I love finding more organised, efficient processes too. So, many of the roles left me bored. Do you find that sometimes? I'd much rather be at home searching charity shops, having my hair done, getting my lip waxed without worrying about going back into a boring office, doing the errands I'd usually have to do at the weekend, buying a packet of biscuits and sitting in front of the telly eating them than sat at work bored because I've already done everything that needed doing.

In early 2011 I was managing a team of eleven administrators, as well as working as a PA for a director, for a national charity. It was great, I had loads to do, but then things suddenly started to get really difficult. Tasks I'd done every day previously I could no longer remember how to do. I'd have a meeting with someone in the morning, then an hour later I'd forgotten everything about it, I'd even forgotten I'd had a meeting.

It was now late 2011 and I knew something wasn't quite right. Hell, I'd lived with myself for 34 years – things were a bit weird. My memory was going, my periods had stopped, I was sweating like mad at night and there were other symptoms, but like I say my memory was going and I kept forgetting what they were.

In 2012, after a year of telling the GP I wasn't bloody stressed and wasn't going through early menopause, it was something more sinister, I was diagnosed with a pituitary tumour. I am sure you know that the pituitary gland sits at the base of our brains and basically controls every facet of our bodies and of our everyday life. It's where our hormones sit and play all day and we all know that without some hormones life can be a bit odd.

In November 2012 I had neurosurgery in Oxford to get the blighter out. If nothing else, it made me realise those cartoons from when I was a kid were nonsense. I'm not invincible.

I spent the next year or two so grateful for life and everything I had. I met my boyfriend in 2013 and fell in love with him and with my daughter all over again.

Fast track to 2014 and I could feel 'something wasn't quite right' again. There was the strange off-balance feeling I'd been getting in 2011. Like when you step out of a lift and it takes a while to find your centre or when you're a little hungry, I was getting it again. Then the night sweats began and my speech became affected as I couldn't remember words easily. I remember having an interview for a promotion with my then-employers. I was earmarked for the job as the interviewers knew me, but I didn't get it because I couldn't recall anything. They all sat there open-mouthed wondering what was wrong with me. The bugger was back!

In June 2014 I had Gamma Knife Radiotherapy in London (say it in a deep American accent, it sounds cool). It's just one targeted intense zap, as opposed to five days a week for five weeks, I was lucky to have the opportunity to have this procedure. I feel for anyone who has to do the five weeks.

I've since mislaid a few hormones and parts of my brain don't work as well as they probably should but in a way, I am kind of glad it happened as I don't think I'd be where I am today without that experience.

In 2016 I changed my life to accommodate my rare disease and became a business owner, making myself happier and healthier than I ever was as an employee.

I continue to lose a few hormones from time to time and have developed a lifetime condition called Addison's Disease. In a nutshell, my brain no longer produces Cortisol, so I have to take fake Cortisol three times a day to keep me alive. Stress can kill me within 20 minutes, because my brain can't cope with it – even good stress – so no sending me massive gifts! With Addison's comes fatigue and other stuff not even worth mentioning, but being my own boss enables me to manage all of that in a way that would not be possible if I was an employee.

I had all the fear you'd expect from making that leap from employee to business owner; what if I ran out of money? What about a pension (I don't have one anyway, but I decided to worry about it for about a day anyway)? Self-doubt – I can't be a business owner, only people with money are business owners – lie! How will my daughter go to uni? What if I get ill again? Everything was trumped with 'what if my employers made me redundant?'

My journey had to work, so that's why I can confidently share with you my tips and insights into the world of running your own successful virtual assistant business.

If life is getting in the way of your happiness and health, then I hope if nothing else this book proves to you that you too can make changes.

As a virtual assistant I have been featured in *Mail Online, The Independent, Forbes, Metro, The Guardian* and on *BBC Wiltshire.* I like to raise the profile of our profession and raise awareness of my illness so others who may be suffering know it's not the end of enjoying life, in fact it may just be the beginning.

Twitter: DelegateVA / howtobea_va

Facebook: DelegateVA / howtobeava

LinkedIn: DelegateVA

Instagram: DelegateVA / howtobea_va

Printed in Great Britain
by Amazon

22555933R00079